TO CUT A LONG STORY SHORT

RANJAN SEN

Om Books International

First published in 2025 by

Om Books International

Corporate & Editorial Office
A-12, Sector 64, Noida 201 301
Uttar Pradesh, India
Phone: +91 120 477 4100
Email: editorial@ombooks.com
Website: www.ombooksinternational.com

Sales Office
107, Ansari Road, Darya Ganj,
New Delhi 110 002, India
Phone: +91 11 4000 9000
Fax: +91 11 2327 8091
Email: sales@ombooks.com
Website: www.ombooks.com

ISBN: 978-93-63951-02-0

Printed in India

10 9 8 7 6 5 4 3 2 1

Ranjan Sen was born and schooled in what was then Calcutta. He read economics in and completed an MBA from Delhi University, winning a slew of public-speaking awards along the way while working as a radio jockey and writing features for national newspapers. This chaotic preparation propelled Ranjan to a three-decade career in international banking across diverse countries in various leadership positions. He has now stepped back from a corporate role to pursue a newfound passion in early-stage investing and to openly romance his childhood sweetheart—writing. His short stories have been published in prestigious international journals like *Kitaab* in Singapore, *The Thieving Magpie* in the US, *The Contemporary Literary Review of India* and the *English Journal of the Sahitya Akademi* in India.

Ranjan's best friend, Manisha, took him on as a husband project many years ago. They currently reside in Delhi with their college-going son, perilously close to many relatives.

To Baba, forever the wind beneath my wings.
And to Ma, the first and most magical storyteller in my life.

Contents

1

The Keeper of Records

I awoke with a start, feeling disoriented, my heart thudding against my chest.

A bulky silhouette loomed in the dark above me, odd shafts of distant lamplight bouncing off his gold chains, intensifying the blood red of his silk *angavastram* and creating shifting shadows around his deep-set eyes and his thick, black oiled moustache.

"Wake up! It is a vital matter, come on now…" Finance Minister Brihadrath said hoarsely in a low, urgent voice as he shook my shoulder.

I blinked, confused. My faithful old servant Kurnoo stood at the foot of my bed, holding a single wick aloft, his eyelids heavy with slumber and ringed by fear. The slow, sonorous clanging of a bell outside and the sound of heavy battle staffs being trundled along the road by the night watch accompanied the calling of the time—it was the third *prahar*, the darkest part of the night.

My throat constricted with anxiety and suddenly I couldn't breathe as a horrible memory crept unbidden across my mind's eye.

It had occurred barely a month ago…

…when the noble Brihadrath had complained to the *Mantrimandal* that the empire's tax revenues were down, I had gently attempted to highlight that the common people were measurably wealthier, while commerce with the southern kingdoms had grown manifold, hence the country expected that the tax revenues would have grown as well.

The honourable finance minister had further demanded that the province of Taxila should do more for the wealth of the empire because it was the trading hub with the world beyond the Hindu Kush mountains. I had felt honour-bound as the keeper of records to point out that the southern province of Suvarnagiri in fact had a greater responsibility to the Empire since it traded with the three powerful allied kingdoms to our South—the Cholas, the Cheras and the Pandyas—which were a flourishing commercial corridor in and of themselves as well as a vital conduit to the eastern kingdoms which lay beyond, all the way to Bali, Java and Siam.

The imperious Brihadrath was not used to any questions from lesser mortals; he had been visibly annoyed by the challenge to his views, as a result of which I had been summarily silenced by the prime minister brusquely raising his palm in my direction, cutting me off in mid-sentence. Belatedly realising my mistake, I had repeatedly tried to apologise to the honourable Brihadrath after the ministerial conclave, but he had swept past me with an angry flourish, flinging his angavastram over his shoulder and striding down the palace steps to his waiting chariot without a backward glance.

I had been left to mull over my own impetuosity, the number of hushed whispers directed towards me adding to my concerns, my anxiety heightened manifold by Brihadrath's steadfast refusal to grant me an audience after that.

As I came back to the present with a start, I realised I was trembling now under the bedsheets, wondering why the finance minister of the mighty Maurya Empire was leaning over me in the dead of the night. His next words, though terrible, relieved me somewhat.

"There's been an assassination," rumbled Brihadrath in the same hushed, urgent tone. "A powerful person has been found in the quarry. Key ministers are investigating before it becomes public, we need the keeper of records with us; come quickly, lad, my chariot awaits."

So saying, he turned on his heel and strode away, clearly expecting me to follow immediately.

It seemed that I really did not have any option.

Kurnoo helped me as I swiftly threw on my clothes and wrapped myself in an outer robe, before taking the narrow stairs two at a time to hurry out of my moderate house. The wintry night wind whistled around the corners and bit into me under a moonless sky as I shivered involuntarily, uncertain of what lay ahead.

My name, dear reader, is Vichitraputra.

When the great emperor Chandragupta Maurya wrested the throne of Magadh from the powerful Nandas, it was made possible by his mentor, the visionary Brahmin Chanakya, who wove an intricate plot to make it all happen. Of the many *chaturanga* pieces he moved around, the last (and some say most vital) element of the great Brahmin's plan was to win over the towering statesman who had served the Nandas as their last prime minister—Rakshasa Katyayan.

There were considerable difficulties, but in the end, the noble Rakshasa Katyayan was indeed successfully won over, and history was made as the victorious Chandragupta ascended the throne of Magadh. In the years and decades after that, Chandragupta Maurya and his prime minister, advised by the incomparable Chanakya, turned an already strong country into the largest and most powerful Empire in the known world. Their kingdom extended from the Hindu Kush Mountains in the west to the hills of Chittagong in the east and from the incomparable valley of Kashmir in the north to the edge of the Deccan kingdoms in the south.

Despite enjoying immense and continued political success, Rakshasa Katyayan's personal life was unfortunately and repeatedly beset with tragedy. His parents died young, his brothers (goaded by his political enemies) allied against him and his sister killed herself. One night while he was away on an early military campaign, his wife perished in a freak fire, along with his three growing children. It was whispered in the brothels and dimly lit narrow by-lanes on the outskirts of the city that Lord Vishnu was isolating the great man, leaving him without close family to build his influence or challenge the nobility or the emperor, forcing him to redirect his immense energies to building the wondrous reign of Chandragupta.

Lord Vishnu it might well have been, but working through the wily Chanakya, a few dared to opine while deep in the thrall of many cups of the sweet *madira* that the rest-houses of Magadh were famous for. But these unfortunate loose-tongued louts with hyperactive imaginations usually disappeared soon after without a trace, as mercenaries and beggars are wont to do, making it clear to even the meanest intelligence that this uncharitable slur on the great Brahmin was a sign of bad luck; no one spoke of it further.

Rakshasa Katyayan was devastated by the string of tragedies, but as the leader of the nobility that served the emperor, he felt he was expected to produce an heir, so he remarried with great ceremony a few years later.

Unfortunately, once again, the gods had something else in mind.

Rakshasa Katyayan once again mourned deeply, and the whole nation with him, when his pregnant new wife's chariot inexplicably tumbled off the road and was smashed amongst rocks in the raging Son one bitter monsoon afternoon. After that, when the Raj Purohit consulted with the stars and advised him that the gods had not written an heir into his destiny, a dispirited Rakshasa Katyayan eschewed marriage forever, throwing all his considerable energy into nation building as per Chandragupta's and Chanakya's vision.

Nevertheless, he was a red-blooded man, complete with all of any normal man's needs and desires. And so it transpired that one summer morning—more than two decades after the noble Chanakya ran into the queen's private quarters with gleaming knives to carve open Emperor Chandragupta's dead wife on the floor of her royal chamber and lift out the blood-stained, premature Bindusara, heir to the royal throne—a humble farmer's daughter serving in the palace kitchens also died, giving birth to me—a bastard son to the Imperial Prime Minister.

I am the only male child sired by the prime minister that I know of, which made me different. While acknowledged by my noble and powerful father and given shelter under his roof, there was no place for me in his social order because I was not the result of a sanctified holy bond of matrimony to an equal, but rather, proof of his baser instincts and moments of weakness with a base-born woman. Coupled with his frequent campaigns with Emperor Chandragupta and his oversight of the distant reaches of the empire, I saw him even more rarely than I sighted a full moon during my formative years.

As a result, I grew up in a lonely world, almost invisible to others—somewhere between the luxurious lives of the noble prime minister's extended family (who didn't wish to be reminded of his tryst with a lowborn woman) and the servants hall, who were forever and always beneath my station.

But my father did give me one priceless piece of support.

In the year that the mighty Emperor Chandragupta gave up his throne to the relentless Bindusara and joined a wandering band of Jain monks, I was accepted into the great Chanakya's Gurukul on Rakshasa Katyayan's personal request.

The noble Brahmin had been surprisingly gracious about the fact that my noble natural father's insistence had gifted me an opportunity that hundreds of others had to compete and fight for.

As he admitted me into his Gurukul, he had gripped my then childish chin in his dry, bony fingers. "I see in you a seed of extraordinary intellect, my boy. As we enter into the time-honoured contract of the *Guru Shishya parampara*, I hereby solemnly swear to teach you all the technical skills of statecraft—mathematics, astronomy, bookkeeping, taxation, public administration, et al.," he uttered solemnly, to my trembling delight.

But with a flash of something impenetrable in his honey-coloured eyes, he had continued, "However… the lessons of politics and the niceties of debate and managing people? Ah, those critical subjects I will leave to your noble and most accomplished birth father to teach you…"

And even though the noble Rakshasa Katyayan rarely spoke to me after that momentous day (far less teach me anything), the Old Master stayed true to his word, teaching me as much and more than he taught my better-born peers, challenging my intellect, drawing out depths of thought and rationality I never knew I possessed, and rewarding me with rare praise that still exceeded the sum total of what all my peers earned.

Right up until the day I put my final *guru dakshina* at his feet, when he commended me one last time for my academic excellence, and in one swift, surprising sentence appointed me as the keeper of records to the Imperial *Mantrimandal*.

I found that every bit of my extensive education came into early use in my huge assignment, as I took over the job from the long-serving but now almost senile Vratistath. I worked night and day for months, carefully going over each task several times, seizing on moments of clarity in the venerable Vratistath to learn all I could, poring over the work of each of the record makers who worked together in the giant windowless rooms in the basement of the Royal Palace. I was proud that by the end of the first monsoon harvest, I was able to gain a tenuous control over most of the vital information that went into the running of this vast Empire and had earned the praise of Emperor Bindusara in open council, no less.

After a lifetime of real and imagined slights, at last I was beginning to feel a sense of belonging. I was in a role that hundreds of the best and most noble in the kingdom aspired to and competed for. With the demonstration of early results, I truly felt I had been handpicked for the job because of my skills, not because of my father. And I was happier than I had ever been, even though I was still an outsider amongst the nobility, with no real friends or family to distract me from my work.

Sometimes though, in rare moments of despondency, I felt that the gap in understanding politics and debates and the art of persuading people in my education could impede my success, as it seemed to have done in the incident with Brihadrath. But I was determined to learn quickly from my mistakes. And indeed, an opportunity arose a few weeks after the clash with Brihadrath, when the imperial records showed that more messengers from Susima (governor of Taxila on the North Western boundaries of our empire and heir to Emperor Bindusara) had disappeared on the *Uttarapath* (the great road we had constructed to bind the empire across future generations) to Pataliputra in the past six months than in three years prior to that. Instead of blurting out this disturbing news in a wider council, I cannily sought a separate audience with the venerable Advaita, minister for roadways.

The white-haired and beringed old nobleman was clearly caught unawares by the information, but I was encouraged by the fact that he heard me out patiently. He did confess he had not thought about it and didn't have a ready answer, but he readily acknowledged my reading that it was a real concern and promised to look into it, which to me represented my own progress in politics and people management.

I wanted my contribution to the empire to be my redemption, my atonement for my bastard birth… And now, I was teaching myself to complete my education. So I had begun to feel a little more confident that I could live up to my illustrious father's accomplishments, maybe build on his power and even leave a legacy…

Maybe starting tonight…

I found Brihadrath's ceremonial chariot outside, with the curtains drawn and the lead lamps burning low. The muscular young charioteer with shaved head, Adhuna, who knew me well, jumped down and touched my feet in a ceremonious *pranaam*, then assisted me respectfully as I climbed the steep steps.

I was somewhat taken aback to find a third person already ensconced in the deep, plush seats of the carriage—the sage old minister of culture and ceremonies was already inside, bundled in multiple colourfully crafted robes. Kanakadhar was always cheerful and one of the elders who continued to educate me with his experience, having served successfully under three different kings. His narrow black eyes twinkled above his flowing white beard as I bent in respectful pranaam; he took my arm in an avuncular manner and pulled me in to sit beside him.

Brihadrath sat opposite, looking a lot less fierce and surprisingly more tired now in the dim starlight. He passed me a narrow-necked earthen jar and said in a gruff, encouraging tone, "Drink deeply, lad, we need all the warmth we can get tonight."

As I took a deep swallow of *madira* mulled with cloves and cinnamon, the carriage set off with a jerk.

My humble house was located in an anonymous cul de sac at the end of the grand Rajpath, which led to the royal palace, befitting my station as a neophyte on the edge of acceptance. The carriage trundled off up the Rajpath through a veil of mist that had crept in from the Son, the Gandaka and the Ganga, the three great rivers that bound our magnificent fortified city state of Pataliputra. It was mingled with woodsmoke from the many small fires lit by the poor to warm themselves, so visibility was down to a few carriage lengths and sounds reverberated eerily through the smoky, misty darkness.

Our horse's hooves were wrapped in thick jute bags to muffle their sound; we heard a few stray dogs, the calling out of the night watch, the creaking of wooden structures in the wind, faint voices apparently raised in argument and even the faraway sound of drunken singing, but it was impossible to determine whence they came.

The horses slowed and then stopped at one of the largest mansions on Rajpath, close to the royal palace. A tall, heavily covered figure was already waiting in the darkness, his shadow reaching out ahead of him in distorted fragments through the smoky mist. The carriage tilted and swayed as he climbed in and I bent in deep *pranaam* again to Shashigupta, the powerful minister of defence.

He was a man of few words, whom I admired greatly. When my record keepers worked on a census of the army earlier this year, I had spent a lot of time with Shashigupta. Because war elephants were dangerous and their mahouts were contemptuous of record keepers, there had never been a complete census of these valued beasts. But I had devised an innovative method of counting them by measuring their total faeces and dividing by a normal value, which interested and amused Shashigupta greatly. Unfortunately, by our accounting standards, it seemed that almost a hundred elephants were unaccounted for, which was no laughing matter, so he had promised to command his mahouts to carry out a formal census.

I wanted to consult him on another matter too. I'd analysed the early reports of the rebellion that our younger prince, Ashoka, had quelled so effectively in Ujjaini. I found the fatal injuries to the rebels inconsistent with the limited cavalry force that Ashoka commanded and I was keen to understand this better.

But in my newfound political wisdom, it struck me that perhaps tonight was not the time.

Shashigupta gratefully accepted the earthen vessel from me, drank deeply and asked Brihadrath the question that had vexed my mind. "Where's the prime minister?"

Brihadrath looked up, his brow furrowed. "We will not disturb Rakshasa Katyayan's sleep at this stage; let's first review what happened. We can brief him at daybreak."

Shashigupta nodded in acknowledgement and leaned back.

We travelled speedily, exiting the walled city through the southernmost of its fifty-odd barricaded gates. The stench of the stagnant water in the giant moat surrounding the colossal wooden walls was quickly left behind. We rattled through the royal highway between rolling farmlands painted silvery black by a starlit sky, on the route to the royal quarry.

When we reached the incline at the edge of the royal quarry, I looked out of the window, past the multiple layers of bamboo scaffolding tied together with hemp ropes to spy another chariot already waiting at the bottom. Our carriage slowed to a walking pace as we descended the sloping entrance road and came to a stop near the other.

We disembarked, stamping our feet in the cold. I recognised the noble Advaita and the minister for palace affairs, Bishakhadatta, standing behind the other carriage, also huddled in the cold. Standing alongside them was a much younger figure, Radhagupte, my classmate from the Gurukul. He came from the noblest of families and was always reputed to be Chanakya's favourite, but given the difference in our birth, we had not been close enough to share any confidences.

I was oddly reassured to see his expression mirroring the same mix of uncertainty and anticipation that I felt. I was not the only one bemused by this assignation in the dead of the night.

Of the quarry workers who normally thronged the site day and night, working with lanterns at night for the enrichment and progress of Magadha, there was no sign. Even their cheap, flickering oil lanterns were scattered and lightless in the dark.

The two parties greeted each other solemnly, gripping one another's forearms and hugging in silence, after which we fell in behind Bishakhadatta, who lit fresh torches and led us into a large cave on the right. Even there, we walked in order of our palace rank, with Radhagupte and I bringing up the rear together. The charioteers stayed outside.

We gathered inside the mouth of the cave, looking around the high ceilings disappearing into the dark and at

Bishakhadatta expectantly. A long moment passed in silence, and then the darkness at the back of the cave shimmered, took shape and a diminutive figure with a shaved pate stepped into the light.

With a quiver of excitement down my spine, I realised that the Old Master was among us!

Chanakya's tawny eyes bore into each of ours in silence, as if searching for something, and then he started to speak in a low, clear authoritative voice, unmarked by his advanced age.

"Growth is the secret of life, as I have taught many of you personally. Humans, animals, civilisations, institutions—even empires—need to grow. If they stop, they wither and die..." he began without so much as an introduction.

"Our empire is fortunate to have been led by great warriors, who grew it constantly. Chandragupta was unparalleled...and Bindusara outstripped all my expectations... But Susima?"

He paused and his words hung in the air, punctuated by the low-pitched sizzle of the oil lanterns burning.

"He is the heir to the throne, true, however he is...just... an administrator. He is not the leader, the warrior, the creator of growth that his younger brother Ashoka is..."

The group of powerful men around me shifted uncomfortably on their feet at this. My own eyes widened involuntarily. Denigrating the Crown Prince? Was that not treason?

The great Brahmin drew a deep breath. "And so, something has to be done."

The little group surrounding him seemed to collectively let out their breath together; the sound of released breath was audible, causing the lanterns to flicker briefly, sending our shadows cavorting in a macabre dance along the rocky floor and wall.

"To strengthen his image as a war general, a hundred elephants were secretly provided to Ashoka over a period of weeks, so that he could quell the Ujjaini revolt. Taxes collected by Susima's men from Taxila have been quietly rerouted, for some time now, secretly to my old students in Taxila who oppose Susima and seek to challenge his rule, who are against his future ascension to the throne.

"Messengers from Susima's administrators communicating the challenges they face, asking for help…have been… carefully disposed of…so that Bindusara's Mantrimandal is starved of intelligence and the seed of suspicion can be quietly sowed…"

The Great Teacher stopped speaking and lifted his head to look directly at me. "But you had already worked that out, had you not, young Vichitraputra?" He asked with a knowing little smile.

Friendly hands pushed me forward as I mumbled an incoherent response, taken by surprise.

Chanakya started to pace deliberately up and down on the uneven floor of the cave.

"Soon, there will be a revolt in Taxila, which will be widely recognised to have been caused by Susima's maladministration. And Ashoka will ride with his army to tackle the empire's biggest challenge, which will firmly position him to replace Susima as the heir apparent…"

I stole a glance around the group, who were all staring intently at the Great Teacher, mesmerised. I realised with a sudden feeling of belonging that the great Brahmin was plotting again on the magnificent stage of the empire and this time, I was a part of his grand plan. But I was troubled by a set of questions gnawing at the back of my mind: What about my father? Was he a part of this? What did I owe him?

I knew I needed Chanakya's guidance on this.

"There was but one risk, an unknown element, who could have spoken too soon and ruined the empire's future..." said Chanakya, stopping next to Radhagupte. "But he was bludgeoned to death in this very cave by a heavy rock tonight!"

"What rock?" Radhagupte asked in a strangled voice, looking around.

"This one," said Brihadrath behind me.

I turned to see him bringing down a large jagged rock hard on my head.

And then everything went black, forever.

History records that Taxila revolted against Susima's maladministration. Fresh from his subjugation of the Ujjaini rebels, Ashoka ruthlessly beat down the Taxila revolt. Backed by popular opinion and Rakshasa Katyayan's successor, Radhagupte, Ashoka brutally assassinated Susima to win the right to ascend the throne of the Maurya Empire after Bindusara.

2

The Edge of Violence

The high-ceilinged, expensively decorated hotel lobby was awash with clear, winter sunlight as the huge bay windows looked out on the deep blue seas off the Goan coast. There was a hum of cheerful activity as the wedding planners of the Sisodia-Bagrodia union attended to incoming guests and escorted them to their rooms, replete with welcome hampers full of goodies, garlands of scented flowers and a schedule of entertainment and appointments for the rest of their stay.

European, Middle Eastern and North American guests floating through the lobby stopped to enjoy the exotic sights—the rich ethnic outfits, the profusion of flower arrangements, the *teeka* ceremony, the bouncy welcome dhol rhythm and the sheer warmth and *joi de vivre* of the coming together of two large Indian families—many of the foreigners stopped to ask questions or take photographs.

The hotel's front desk staff were occupied with their regular duties, relatively undisturbed by the wedding arrangements, tending courteously to their steady flow of wealthy guests as the wedding planners took care of the marriage invitees.

It was the bellboy near the lift who heard it first, a distant shriek that grew ominously closer as one of the main elevators descended smoothly towards them. As it neared the lobby, the disturbing high-pitched screaming crept through the crowd insidiously, dampening the festivity swiftly and repressively like a dark cloud slowly casting a creeping shadow over the gathered people, until the whole floor fell silent, waiting for the doors to open and reveal the horror inside.

It had all started way back in 1976, under a monsoon sky on a lonely, meandering road leading to Calcutta.

A white flash of lightning ripped the grey, cloudy sky into jagged fragments as the accompanying thunder rumbled deeply, rolling away towards the rain-soaked horizon.

S.K. Babu disembarked from his shining black Mercedes with the help of his faithful driver as two well-used white Ambassador cars behind him disgorged a number of his men, sporting the rolled sleeves and brawny arms which indicated their profession. He had been summoned by an urgent phone call from the nearby post office, so he had some idea of what he was walking into. His measured, deliberate glance moved slowly from his three trucks which were incongruously standing idle in the middle of the road, to his three truck drivers squatting nearby with blood-spattered shirts and battered faces, coming around slowly to rest on the large group of youth gathered under a party flag on the side of the asphalt, raucously drinking out of tin cups.

"Who is in charge? Why have my trucks been stopped?" S.K. Babu asked in the authoritative manner of one used to having his commands obeyed. His voice was calm and steady, but the rigidity of his shoulders and back betrayed his tension.

The group of youngsters insolently ignored S.K. Babu and continued their boisterous conversation, but one of the young men separated himself from the group and walked quietly towards S.K. Babu. He was tall, with shrewd deep-set eyes and the inevitable long hair copied from Hindi film icons of the times. Unlike his lean colleagues, he seemed to have invested considerably in building his physique, with strong muscles evident under his partially unbuttoned shirt.

He stopped a few yards from S.K. Babu, a non-threatening distance intended to convey respect.

"Shaheb, nomoshkaar."

S.K. Babu nodded politely in acknowledgement, but did not say anything. He was an old hand at dealing with recalcitrant Bengali youth; he knew better than to rush headlong into any confrontation or reveal his hand first.

There was a long moment of silence, while both men sized each other up. S.K. Babu turned back briefly and in response to the unspoken signal, his men walked a few steps forward and stood behind him.

The tall young man took in the gesture and a boyish grin tugged at the corners of his mouth. Far from being intimidated, he was apparently enjoying this.

"Shaheb, can I say that your men had three chances?" He said in steady voice, pitched loud enough so that it carried all the way to his men as well.

S.K. Babu tilted his head questioningly, but did not say anything.

The tall youngster ticked off actions on his fingers. "First, when the party announced this bandh, we told everybody we had loudspeakers on rickshaws, even the radio news covered it. Second, when we put up posters all over Bengal, everybody saw it; and again, third when I personally visited your garage and explained to them that they need to stay off the roads today." He stopped for a dramatic pause and then splayed out his hands. "What more could I have done?"

He glanced back at his group of party workers, who had fallen silent and now were listening keenly to the exchange; he squared his shoulders and looked S.K. Babu in the eye. "Tell me, Shaheb, after this, the consequences are their responsibility, na? If Jhontu Ghosh lets them go after this, neither the party nor the public will trust me again."

Jhontu seemed to have deliberately separated the actions of the men from the decisions of their master, offering S.K. Babu a face-saving opportunity to rise above the conflict. The slight relaxation of S.K. Babu's posture grudgingly acknowledged thc rational tone and the proffered opportunity.

Sensing an opening, Jhontu stepped in and spoke softly so that his men could not overhear. "If you leave now, we will look like we have protected the sanctity of the bandh. But your trucks don't have to go back, I will keep them here and release them after dark. I will get some of my trusted boys to accompany the drivers, who can drive them through the night to make sure they reach their destination tomorrow morning…"

Struck by the simplicity of the solution and realising that a potentially violent conflict could be completely avoided,

S.K. Babu nodded almost imperceptibly and replied in an equally soft voice, “Come and meet me.” After which, he stepped back in an exaggerated gesture and for the sake of both sides, protested indignantly for several minutes about the harassment of honest businessmen and threatened police action while Jhontu feigned arrogant indifference, hands in pockets.

S.K. Babu then turned abruptly on his heel, stopping to speak briefly to his drivers before leading his little cavalcade back to Kolkata.

Jhontu Ghosh eventually did go to meet S.K. Babu.

Not after just a day or even a week, that would have shown undue keenness and would have placed him in a weak negotiating position, but within the month.

After all, Subodh Kanti Aggrawal was a powerful construction company owner, a respected figure in the Marwari business community and came from a pedigreed, wealthy family… Not a man to be ignored or trifled with.

A couple of uniformed watchmen stopped the tall young man at a huge wrought-iron gate, through which he could see manicured lawns surrounded by flowering bushes and a multitude of trees, almost hiding the large mansion beyond them. As word was delivered from the house that babu would see the visitor, he tried hard not to be impressed by the opulence.

S.K. Babu had over the years developed an unshakeable faith in his own ability to instantly judge character, born as he had been to commanding wealth and having overseen a plethora of domestic and professional subordinates from an early age.

He unhesitatingly offered the young party foot soldier a job.

Jhontu had been expecting some sort of a surreptitious cash reward and was taken aback by the sudden job offer. He pursed his lips thoughtfully and promised to think about it, before taking his leave.

While he battled with his conscience and party commitments over the next few days, S.K. Babu cannily upped the ante and had his men bring Jhontu's widowed mother before him so that he could benevolently inform her of the offer of a regular salary for her eldest son, promising to complete his education and offering her family the financial security and legitimacy that all her neighbours were struggling for.

Jhontu as a quintessential young Bengali man had no defence against his mother's wishes. And thus masterfully outflanked by superior tactics, Jhontu migrated from enforcing communist policy in rural Bengal to facilitating construction development in and around the great metropolitan city of Calcutta in the tumultuous 1970s.

Jhontu was not just very good with his fists, but also with words; add to this a school education till the eighth standard, a curious mind and a quick grasp which helped him learn the key business levers quickly. He didn't waste time becoming a potent force in his new role.

On several occasions, Jhontu turned up at the gates of S.K. Babu's palatial mansion in Alipore with news of upcoming labour unrest or changes in competitors, offering streetwise advice on how to turn these issues to their company's advantage, which made S.K. Babu sit up and take further notice of him.

Jhontu moved up the chain of command swiftly in the next few years, while assiduously educating himself in night classes organised by S.K. Babu, who saw in this young man a powerful and sophisticated weapon of enforcement in the disorganised and unstable construction business.

Jhontu also used S.K. Babu's resources to build on his old party connections, from which he benefited smartly, whether through advance notice on legislation or on routing and logistics of the upcoming Metro rail or even prior access to striking workers. On his part, Jhontu ensured that all the relevant palms were greased, meticulously recording details down to the serial numbers of notes, to ensure that S.K. Babu always had full and transparent information.

In the normal course, Jhontu would no doubt have continued his growth in the construction industry as an able field manager, enriching his family and friends and in time building his own coterie of enforcers.

But Fate had something else in mind.

❧

It was in 1984 when the short-lived autumn was ceding ground to a gently incoming winter that Jhontu Ghosh's life became forever and inextricably intertwined with the Aggrawal family's.

They were travelling to the airport on Delhi's Outer Ring Road after a successful meeting with senior government bureaucrats when the news of Indira Gandhi's assassination broke out. Unbeknownst to the little travelling party, havoc broke out across the city and their black Mercedes was set upon by a rampaging mob who were stopping traffic and attacking wealthy car owners, their passions further inflamed by the sight of S.K. Babu's customary pagri.

Smashing windows with steel pipes and pushing their arms in to wrench doors open, the jeering, screaming crowd hauled S.K. Babu and his driver out. S.K. Babu's daughter, Sangeeta, who had accompanied him for this important meeting, vainly tried clinging to him to keep him in the car, pleading hysterically as the mob overwhelmed her.

In his normal front seat next to the driver, Jhontu's street-fighting instincts immediately took over. He manoeuvred desperately to get into the driver's seat while fending off the grasping hands reaching inside the car, slashing destructively with the flick knife he always carried; as he fell into the driving seat, he slammed down his foot, flooring the accelerator. The big, expensive car responded with a roar of urgency, barrelling brutally through the crowd to emerge to a clear road ahead. The howling mob set off after them, but the car easily lost them in the rear-view mirror, leaving them panting helplessly as they gave up the chase.

A few kilometres after reversing their direction, Jhontu turned into the posh old colony of Hauz Khas Enclave, with Sangeeta still hysterically shrieking in the backseat. The car stuttered to a standstill as he dragged up the handbrake and turned to reason with Sangeeta.

But she was well beyond words at that stage. As her crazed, unresponding eyes swivelled past him in a paroxysm of fear, her hands hammered the seats; deaf to his entreaties, she continued sobbing and screaming between long shuddering breaths.

Jhontu continued trying to calm her down for a few minutes, then reached a decision and sharply slapped her twice across her face. Sangeeta was suddenly shocked into a whimpering, hiccupping silence as he dragged her by the arm and knocked repeatedly on the nearest door, which was opened after a while by a protective middle-aged man holding a hockey stick, with his teenaged sons behind him.

Jhontu roughly thrust the shivering Sangeeta at them. "There has been a violent riot," he rasped.

The householder nodded slowly, taking in the wild-eyed, expensively dressed girl and the tall, intense young man with blood on his arms and ripped shirt, with the badly damaged Mercedes on the road.

"Please look after her, she is at breaking point," Jhontu continued, "I have to go..."

Then Jhontu turned to run back for S.K. Babu.

The mob had raged on and flowed away towards a new target, but there were smaller angry groups of men armed with a motley assortment of rods, sticks, swords and hockey sticks roaming the roads. They all gave the tall muscular man with bloody arms a wide berth as he half walked and half jogged down the Outer Ring Road, calling out for S.K. Babu. Jhontu finally found him lying in a gutter after almost two hours, the older man's right arm and several ribs broken, his rotund torso leaking blood from multiple gashes.

Jhontu did not stop to think whether he would exacerbate any internal wounds; he picked up the battered older man and carried him down the road on his back till he found an autorickshaw to drive them through inside roads to the AIIMS. S.K. Babu had lost a great deal of blood and was in intense agony, but the seasoned old veteran was not done yet. Going in and out of consciousness, he still clung stubbornly to life through the dangerous, bumpy ride, through several hours of surgery and through months of recuperative therapy, thereafter to recover full strength in less than a year after the horrific incident.

Sangeeta was S.K. Babu's only child, the apple of his eye and the sole heir to his entire fortune. S.K. Babu and his wife had made great plans for their talented young daughter, who had received the best education possible from the prestigious Loretto College in Calcutta and topped off with an economics degree from the London School of Economics. They wanted her to marry into a another, equally or preferably even more powerful Marwari family so as to join the two businesses and strengthen the standing of both families, while of course, adding a firm male hand on the tiller of S.K. Babu's own business interests.

Sangeeta had always been completely in tune with her parents. The only thing was, they had not accounted for this dramatic turn of events which would turn their lives upside down.

After surviving the trauma of the mob, Sangeeta not only felt she owed Jhontu her life, she was in fact overcome by a schoolgirl adoration of his strength and courage; so much so that she became completely obsessed with Jhontu, with her feelings only being strengthened by her parents' disapproval.

"He saved me, this man risked his own life to save me from rape and murder—why does that not matter to you?" She would emotionally throw back at her parents as they remonstrated with her. "Papa is alive only because of Jhontu, but you don't care, you don't care! You are only worried about the opinions of strangers!"

S.K. Babu was in his heart already beholden to Jhontu and admired the young man, although more as an exceptional employee rather than as a family member. But this place in his heart for Jhontu played its part, as after a few months of intense debate within the wider family where Sangeeta's resolve showed no signs of weakening, S.K. Babu gave in despite the horrified protestations of his wife and family, and married Sangeeta off to Jhontu.

It was a lavish and traditional affair, attended by business and political luminaries from Bengal and as far afield as Dhaka, Delhi and Mumbai. But there were also many powerful and conservative Marwari families who chose to stay away; and there was a malicious whisper campaign about Sangeeta marrying in desperation below her station in life, which greatly saddened S.K. Babu, but never deterred him for a moment.

Despite the many challenges leading up to their marriage, the newlyweds enjoyed their honeymoon in exotic Singapore (lovingly arranged by S.K. Babu) and upon returning, quickly settled into their own unique rhythm.

For the first few years, Jhontu threw himself during the day into managing the increased responsibility which came his way as the heir apparent to S.K. Babu's business, while Sangeeta invested every evening educating him about social niceties, global economic views, national and Bengali political themes, art, fine dining and a myriad other things which were as natural to her upbringing as they were new and alien to Jhontu.

He on his part gratefully saw her as the opportunity of a lifetime and was careful and gentle with her, but still primitive and sexual as he was with all women, which seemed to suit Sangeeta, who responded passionately. And their union bore fruit within a year in the form of their first daughter, Vaidehi.

The construction business prospered tremendously under Jhontu, although stories abounded about intimidation of small landowners and payoffs to senior government officials. Other instances when Jhontu's primal instincts led to his fists talking were quickly and expensively hushed up, sometimes needing the intervention of S.K. Babu himself as a trusted elder statesman. It seemed that Jhontu's insatiable hunger for success and his natural street instincts always perched him on the edge of violence.

Sangeeta and Jhontu were blessed with a second daughter, Brinda, two years later. This time Jhontu had been keenly looking forward to a son and was visibly disappointed; but he was nevertheless dutiful and present throughout the birth and the weeklong ceremonies that followed, smiling through the celebrations before slipping off back to his work, leaving Sangeeta starting to feel a bit alone.

The truth was that Jhontu's success felt incomplete.

Even as his commercial success multiplied, Jhontu found to his chagrin that a number of doors still remained implacably closed to him. He was not always invited to all the major weddings that S.K. Babu continued to be warmly welcomed at; he sat two rows behind business owners and professional corporate leaders in industry body and chambers of commerce events; he knocked on a number of doors but unfortunately couldn't even find proposers and seconders to support his bid for membership of the posh Calcutta Club or Bengal Club…all of which meant that he continued to remain an outsider to the core business community in the city and the state, an outlier in terms of informal information, always struggling to access the biggest and most lucrative contracts, tolerated by the best families but never fully a part of their lives.

In the early days, it did not bother him as he did not even understand or recognise the gap for what it was. He invested all his considerable energies into building the business that S.K. Babu was slowly handing over to him. But as time progressed and his understanding of his new world grew deeper, Jhontu began to chafe at the chasm between him and Sangeeta's social peer group. Try as he might, he knew that he had limitations of language, education and birth which would never fully enable him to fit in with the privileged wealthy families whose children were born into it—but as he began to appreciate the difference that birth made, he became increasingly optimistic that maybe the next generation of his family would be able to break down these invisible barriers.

He knew daughters could not unlock the doors of this elusive, male-dominated world which was just out of his reach. So Jhontu started to privately obsess about having a son through whom his own standing could be legitimised.

He had nurtured great hopes when Sangeeta became pregnant for the second time, but it was not to be. After their second daughter was born, he started to become progressively more impatient, consulting the best known doctors in the field and putting Sangeeta through multiple medical examinations; he even visited religious shrines and tried a number of absurd and challenging sexual positions advised by quacks and charlatans in his bid to sire a male heir.

Many a times, Sangeeta watched fearfully as his brooding, morose silence turned into violent breakages of crockery and household knickknacks and sometimes into an open-handed slap for an unfortunate male servant. So it was with as much relief as happiness that she welcomed a third child into the world after another almost three years—their son, Rishaan.

Rishaan was a sweet, gentle and obedient child from his very infancy. With his father's hazel eyes, his mother's fair complexion and his own unique dimpled smile, he charmed their family and friends and especially was irresistible to ladies of all ages, from S.K. Babu's wife and his doting grandmother to his little sisters. Born into wealth and privilege, he was also blessed with empathy for the less fortunate, a good-natured child who was kind to everyone he knew, without exception.

S.K. Babu himself was overjoyed about his grandson. "I love you both so much," he told his two little granddaughters who clutched his hands tightly as they welcomed Rishaan and Sangeeta home from the hospital. "But now, our family is truly complete!"

There was a lavish celebration to commemorate this advent of a male heir, followed by exceptional arrangements for the little child, including an absurdly expensive English nanny, imported all the way from Hong Kong.

No expense was spared in little Rishaan's upbringing, as both his father and his grandfather were raising him to succeed in an increasingly competitive world.

Through his many contacts, S.K. Babu secured Rishaan's admission into the most prestigious school in the city—La Martiniere for Boys. Whether he was keen on it or not, Rishaan found himself participating in every activity considered appropriate at school and in the various clubs where his parents and grandparents were members—he rode, swam, played cricket, squash and the guitar, tried out for the debate team, joined the Mock UN, studied hard.

He was never a laggard and generally got on well with the inhabitants of all the different worlds he was asked to straddle. But the thing was, he was never at the forefront of any of these activities, though seemingly competent but never quite mustering the intensity to challenge the best.

Jhontu was extremely proud at first and watched fondly from a distance, but started to get more involved and pushed Rishaan harder as he grew older. He knew his son was spared the many hard knocks he had suffered in his own childhood, but he was ambivalent about whether that was a good thing as Rishaan seemed to lack the edge that had served his father so well.

Jhontu desperately wanted his son to excel, although he didn't know quite how to inspire or motivate him, especially in a privileged world that had been denied to him in his own childhood. So he fell back on the only heavy-handed discipline that he knew. Many a night, during his teens, Rishaan went to bed nursing a swollen cheek or ears or a heavily bruised arm as his father's desperation tipped over the edge of violence.

"Baba loves you very much, my dearest," Sangeeta would console her sniffling son, stroking his head. "He is just worried about you, you know," she would say, trying to explain away her husband's brutal behaviour to the frightened little boy.

Rishaan graduated in the top half of his class, which was unfortunately not good enough for elite Indian colleges in

Delhi or Calcutta. Jhontu used all his wealth and resources to research overseas colleges and, with the guidance of the now ailing but still powerful S.K. Babu and the best counsellors and tutors that money could buy, Rishaan eventually went off to the prestigious New York University to study journalism—not the course anyone would have chosen, but it was NYU after all.

In his freshman semester, Rishaan abruptly discovered the joys of breath-taking, unsupervised freedom. Of course, he wrote dutifully home to his parents about the many people he met and the many new things he experienced, but he did not, could not explain everything that happened to him.

Like the headstrong, beautiful and creative Kiara Williams, half English, half Austrian, and fully wild.

And that was when his life changed.

It was instant attraction for both of them. Kiara opened Rishaan's senses to a whole new adventurous, sensory world, taking him rock climbing, to underground music concerts, introducing him to his first stick of marijuana and making love to him in shadow-shifting firelight on the beach. Her exciting presence in his young life imbued Rishaan with an exhilarating self-confidence he'd never experienced before.

In his second semester, Rishaan slowly started to write about Kiara in emails and on WhatsApp to his now married sisters and his mother, hesitantly at first and more adoringly as time went by, even talking blushingly about her when he Skyped them. "She is amazing… Everything that I am not, you know, Ma. She is so worldly-wise, quite fearless, so uninhibited. She is making me a different person!" He would say, causing his mother and sisters to exchange a flurry of worried messages between themselves in the background, while lovingly asking him to be careful.

Notwithstanding his excitement, Rishaan always remained deeply conscious of his father's expectations, so while sharing Kiara with the three adoring women in his life, he exhorted them all the while not to tell Jhontu.

And knowing Jhontu as they did, hoping that Rishaan's infatuation would blow over, they faithfully kept his secret.

Around the time that Rishaan had gone to college, the winds of political change had begun to blow in Bengal. Ever the opportunist, Jhontu had spotted the chance to rebuild his image and had relentlessly courted the upcoming Opposition with all the wealth and muscle power at his disposal. During a discreet conclave at the Opposition leader's home, Jhontu found himself seated for several hours next to one of her staunchest followers, cement baron O.P. Sisodia, with whom he struck up a comfortable rapport as the evening progressed, which carried over into subsequent gatherings.

Whether the brains of the Opposition had conspired with S.K. Babu to plan this coming together or not, Jhontu was deeply gratified with this burgeoning friendship because the old-money Sisodias were practically Calcutta nobility; and because it was the first time he had been thus acknowledged outside of work.

As the Opposition came into power in the next elections, Jhontu's business empire grew discreetly more powerful in a few shared projects with the Sisodias. His personal friendship with O.P. Sisodia deepened, and they along with S.K. Babu began to meet more frequently at each other's family functions until one day, S.K. Babu gently pronounced, "My friends, I am now in the evening of my life…" As the gathered family members demurred, he waved an affectionate hand and continued, "Oh yes, it has been a great journey and I have done most things I wanted. Now, before I go, it is my dearest wish to see OP's granddaughter Diya married to my grandson Rishaan." S.K. Babu finished the little speech he had rehearsed with Jhontu.

O.P. Sisodia stood up with portentous gravity and warmly embraced S.K. Babu in agreement, and the matter was decided.

However, to give the young ones a sense of control over their own destiny, which seemed to be what they wanted nowadays, both the families lovingly plotted to throw Rishaan and Diya together at the upcoming Sisodia family destination wedding in Goa before the big announcement to their family and friends.

❧

Rishaan was devastated when his mother told him he had to meet Diya at the wedding.

"Come on, Ma," he burst out when Sangeeta spoke to him, "you know I have planned this white-water rafting holiday in Rishikesh for all my US college mates? You know that Kiara is coming for the first time? How can I cancel all of that? It will be so awful to ditch so many people!"

He argued with his mother several times and complained to his sisters, but in the end he reluctantly agreed, as they had all known he would.

He still didn't know how to be honest with his father.

Rishaan was indeed deeply disappointed, but through long years of practice, he was able to play off Sangeeta's guilt by negotiating concessions from her—the big one being that their family home would host all his US friends before they travelled to Rishikesh and that he could travel to Goa a couple of days later than the rest of the marriage party. Sangeeta in turn cannily extracted from him the promise that he would come a few days early to Calcutta to meet family friends—including the Sisodias and especially Diya.

When they finally did meet, Diya took Rishaan's breath away. She was petite, ethereal, highly adventurous and, to his utter surprise, already and candidly completely smitten with him—she confessed she'd had a crush on him since she had been in middle school. Rishaan was fully prepared to be aloof and distant, but when Diya cuddled up to him on the darkened veranda and confidentially shared scandalous stories of how she had nearly ruined the family's reputation in her first year of studies at Warwick university in the UK and followed it up with a warm, lingering goodnight kiss, his pre-decided resistance started to crumble a little bit.

The wedding group departed for Goa the next day, with Rishaan's college friends arriving en masse a few hours later. After a couple of nights of partying and painting Kolkata red, Rishaan was at the airport, charming the check-in clerk to print Kiara's boarding pass while she was in the toilet, when he was disconcerted to suddenly find Diya and her dimpled smile behind him, asking for the seat next to his.

She had apparently changed her flight to travel with him.

She was somewhat taken aback when Rishaan accepted a business-class boarding pass for the window seat next to his aisle seat, but she quietly accepted the seat across the aisle.

Sometime during the flight, a still hungover Kiara woke up to go to the washroom again. When she returned, she was not too happy to find that Rishaan had, in her absence, offered her window seat to Diya, who was keen to enjoy the vista of the sun-dappled ocean as the giant airborne ship began its graceful descent towards Goa. With about half an hour still remaining for the flight to land, a sleep-starved Kiara took another power nap, this time holding Rishaan's right hand possessively across the aisle. Rishaan dutifully curled his fingers around Kiara's strong fingers, though his other hand nervously moved to touch Diya's. She looked down at his hand, a little confused by his moodiness, but did not push it away.

When the flight landed in the sweltering midday heat at Dabolim Airport in Goa, Rishaan went through the airport formalities in an absent-minded manner. He had been looking forward to exploring Goa with Kiara, but now, he felt he was being torn in different directions.

Diya had by this time recovered her poise. She chatted animatedly during the airport procedures, then sat next to Rishaan on the limousine to the hotel, relegating a sulky Kiara to the front seat next to the driver. Rishaan found himself responding warmly, even affectionately, to Diya, recognising an amazing number of common interests and shared history in Diya's words, which kept him thoroughly engaged.

Diya stayed beside him through the hotel check-in and happily joined him as the receptionist showed him to his room. As the door closed, Diya stepped in and linked her arm through his. "I know that this has been set up, Rishaan, but I'm getting a really good feeling about the whole alliance," she confided in him cheerfully.

Before he could respond, there was a knock on the open door. Rishaan looked up to find Kiara on the threshold, along with a bellboy carrying the rest of their bags. She took in the scene with narrowed eyes and reacted in her usual mercurial manner. "What the hell is happening here, Rishaan? Why did you leave me in the lobby by myself? Why are you encouraging this rich bitch to paw you all over?"

Rishaan jerked away nervously from Diya and shook his head. "You really shouldn't speak that way," he told Kiara.

Diya stepped in closer, suddenly concerned. "What happened, Rishaan? Have I upset you? I wasn't just talking about the business synergies, I was talking about our relationship," she said in a gentle, lowered tone as she affectionately placed her palms on his chest.

Kiara looked on in disbelief and flung her backpack to the ground with a thump. "What is wrong with you, Rishaan?" She burst out, her voice rising several decibels, almost hysterical now. "Are you going to be bought by her money, like a farm animal? Is that what you brought me all this way to see?"

Rishaan turned away and shook his head violently, his emotions churning.

Diya spontaneously followed him and stepped in close with her head on his chest, to soothe and comfort him.

At that, Kiara went crazy, suddenly lunging at them and shrieking at the top of her lungs, "Get away from her! Get AWAY!"

Rishaan reacted sharply to the uncontrolled rage in Kiara's voice, elbowing Diya away in a violent gesture. Her arms flailed wildly for balance as she tottered back, stumbled over his bags on the floor and smashed down hard on the glass-topped table.

Rishaan stopped for a moment, then nervously took a step towards Diya. His knees suddenly buckled as he saw her sightless eyes and the thick, jagged shard of glass embedded in the back of her head as she lay motionless in a spreading pool of blood.

An hour later, the room was a grim place, filled with people. The grief-stricken Sisodias were weeping inconsolably next to Diya's tarpaulin-covered body, police detectives were questioning all the relatives one at a time, while uniformed constables protected the crime scene and hotel security ensured that everything remained intact.

Rishaan was curled up on the bed, shivering uncontrollably despite the heat, clinging childishly to Sangeeta's hands while Jhontu and a frail S.K. Babu conferred with the assistant commissioner of police overseeing the investigation.

"Where is this Kiara person?" Jhontu demanded in a pent-up, low, intense voice. "Why haven't you questioned her yet? She can confirm what Rishaan said!"

Rishaan started making a low, moaning sound as he sat up and hugged his knees, rocking gently.

The senior policemen looked at him with a strange expression and turned back to Jhontu. "We have checked with everyone, Mr Ghosh—you should know that there is no such person."

That was when Rishaan started screaming.

He was still screaming, his eyes rolling wildly, spittle flowing from his open slack mouth as they strapped him into a white coat and dragged him to the lift.

3

Sacrifice

The eccentric, exotic Priscilla Wang came into their lives while they were having a late and luxurious breakfast together in the beautiful hotel restaurant next to the pool.

It was at the end of their second week in Singapore, the Friday holiday leading into a long weekend. Anand had completed ten productive days at work and had broken ground on the new construction the previous day, which gave him a lot of comfort that he was starting to contribute to his new job in a new company in a new country.

Anand sported shorts and a rugby t-shirt this morning. He had given up being self-conscious about his incipient paunch; he joked that his otherwise spare six-foot frame could carry it off as a symbol of growing success. He was relaxed and smiling as he looked around his family tucking into a hearty morning meal.

Shanta had her long dark hair coiled in a haphazard fashionable pile on top of her head on which her new dark glasses perched. Her heart-shaped face with large dark eyes and striking eyebrows always drew admiring looks; her body language seemed a lot more comfortable than it had been a week ago, although her expression in repose was still somewhat hesitant and wistful.

In truth, Shanta's house-hunting had not gone too well, despite what Anand and she both recognised to be a generous budget from his employers. This bothered her quite a bit, as she saw herself being responsible for making a home for the family. She had been raised in a loving but fairly conservative environment, where the women of the household had defined support roles to play. So, despite her being the eldest of three children, her brothers had claimed their rights to individual bedrooms when they reached their teenaged years while she slept in a cot in her parents' room. And which is why, despite being among the top-ranked in her art course, she was predestined for an arranged marriage after her graduation while the family's savings supported her brothers through their postgraduate course in business and accountancy respectively.

Of course, during the past week, she had gained some confidence through the children's school admissions, which had gone well with both the British and Indian schools.

But it was the two youngest people at the table, Advait and Vaidehi, eleven and nine respectively, who were blissfully oblivious to any stress or worry, enjoying every new sight and sound together in their protected and carefree world. At the moment, they were in a hurry to finish their mandatory morning fruits so they could rush to the chocolate fountain, a novelty which excited them not only as an incredible end to breakfast but as a portent of the fascinating new world to which their parents had introduced them.

A tinkling sound drew their eyes to the uniformed bellboy with the perky pillbox hat, who was walking around with a board while shaking a small handbell.

"Papa, Papa, that's us!" Vaidehi tugged at Anand's hand to get his attention.

Indeed, the board carried by the bellboy carried the words 'Achrekar family—Suite 1104'.

Anand put up his hand to attract the bellboy's attention, a little furrow of concern appearing between his eyebrows—had anything gone wrong? Something about this new life that they were not aware of? "Excuse me please, that is us."

The bellboy trotted over with a polite smile. "Goo' morning, suh. Visitor for you in the lobby, suh," he announced cheerfully.

A small cloud of worry passed over Shanta's face as she looked over at Anand, but he winked back reassuringly at her and squeezed her hand. "Come on, let's go and see who it is."

Leaving the children to the exploration of the chocolate fountain, Shanta followed Anand into the posh hotel lobby as the bellboy led them to a green leather sofa with buttons, where a striking-looking lady of Chinese origin awaited them.

She was very tall, her height further accentuated by stylish high-heeled boots. She had a mane of curly hair, stylishly streaked blonde, framing a strong face with high cheekbones. She rose gracefully and took a couple of steps towards them as she saw them following the bellboy, giving an impression of lithe strength, although she was quite slim and stylishly attired in a pale amber Versace dress with a matching Prada purse.

"Mr Anand Achrekar? Hello, how are you today? My apologies if I have disturbed you and your lovely family on a holiday morning." She smiled and spoke confidently in a low, husky voice while stretching out her hand. "I am Priscilla Wang."

She turned her gaze towards Shanta while shaking a bemused Anand's hand. "And you must be Mrs Achrekar, my dear. If I am honest, I think you are the one that I have come to meet," Priscilla said in a cheerful tumble of words.

As she felt her hand clasped warmly and looked into a pair of sloping, tawny eyes, Shanta instinctively responded to the other woman's effervescence and smiled back a welcome.

"You must be wondering who I am," Priscilla said in response to their quizzical expressions. "Well, I am common friends with Mr Mohammed Yadzi Jidin, whom I believe you know?" She nodded at Anand.

"Ah yes," said Anand with a note of recognition in his voice. He turned to Shanta. "Mr Jidin is the head of HR for the company," he explained.

Priscilla sat down comfortably and invited them to follow, waving the bellboy away imperiously.

It transpired that she owned a bungalow which she was keen to rent out and had been looking for an appropriate tenant. "But I want the right family to live there, you know? It is my home and I need to be comfortable with the family there—and that is not always easy to find…" she said to them confidingly. "If I understand, you are working on the tearing down and the reconstruction of the old coolie quarters near the airport?" She asked, turning to Anand.

"Umm, yes, that is broadly correct," mumbled Anand, put on the spot. He did not know how much of the information was public yet and he did not want to divulge anything confidential.

"Don't worry, I am not going to ask you for details," said Priscilla with a low gurgle of laughter as she noticed his obvious discomfiture. Shanta noticed deep creases appeared around her mouth and eyes when she smiled, suddenly making her look a lot older. But that impression vanished almost as soon as it had appeared.

The children tumbled out of the dining area, their darkly smudged lips a clear giveaway that the short period without parental supervision had been well invested in the chocolate fountain. They were introduced to Priscilla and, to their parents' combined pride, conducted themselves with great aplomb, answering all her questions intelligently and asking several of their own.

"They are absolutely delightful," Priscilla said, turning to Shanta and taking her hands in a warm clasp. "I do really believe the house will be perfect for your little family, my dear—in fact, why don't you come with me and see it now?"

Anand was a little reluctant as he had not yet hired a car and he was always slow to trust people. The children, however, were most enthusiastic to do something with their newfound friend. Particularly Shanta, given her desire to find a home for her family as soon as possible.

Thus, it was agreed that Priscilla would drive them to her bungalow and back for a preliminary visit and after a few minutes to change, they all piled into Priscilla's ancient Range Rover and set off, driving through a confusing combination of main streets and smaller side roads for almost half an hour before driving past a freshly painted high white wall, over the top of which verdant greenery peeped out, and turning off into a charming little private road.

The little road bent at right angles into a break in the high garden wall and turned right again immediately, thereby creating a little protected cul-de-sac just a few metres away from the main road.

There were only two buildings at the end of the little private road. One was a quaint two-storeyed bungalow with sloping red-tiled roofs, large cheerful bay windows and white gables, set back from the road in a nicely landscaped sizeable garden, while the other was a much larger flat-roofed, oblong building with three floors and a more commercial exterior and a grizzled old watchman who nevertheless moved with feline grace to get up and wave back at Priscilla.

The children exclaimed with delight when they saw the bungalow and Shanta was moved to a sudden, relieved smile that lit up her beautiful face. Priscilla herself contentedly basked in reflected glory, enjoying the reactions. It was abundantly clear the little bungalow was very dear to her heart; she was almost purring with joy as she led them in.

There was a spacious and airy drawing room downstairs, a separate dining room, a cosy family lounge and a light-filled, garden-facing kitchen, which lifted Shanta's mood further, with large attached servants quarters for at least three house servants. There were four bedrooms upstairs, the master bedroom leading out to an open terrace overlooking the garden again. It was sparingly furnished, enough for a family to move in but allowing enough leeway for them to add any personal pieces of furniture they wanted to—perfect for the Achrekars, who had only brought a few heavy trunks of kitchen appliances, paintings and knick-knacks with them.

Advait and Vaidehi each loudly laid claim to one of the bedrooms. Anand went around the entire house, assiduously testing the windows and turning the taps on and off.

Priscilla proudly answered the flurry of questions from all of them for almost an hour. The house was over a hundred years old apparently, but it had been modernised by her family and was now fully up to date. The only gap was Wi-Fi, which was to be set up over the coming week.

Anand asked about the building next door and about security. Priscilla confirmed the building next door was owned by a family who used it infrequently and reassured him that this was as safe as anywhere in Singapore; taking him on a tour to show where the house was fitted with all the modern electronic intruder alarms and locking systems.

But there was no doubt about it—the sun-dappled, beautiful, classical bungalow which promised another level of quality of life had taken up the collective imagination of the entire family.

Finally, as they turned to leave, Shanta turned to Anand and told him softly in Marathi, "This is it, Anand, this is it. This is where I see the family. We must have this please, even if it means we make a few sacrifices…"

"Of course, my dear, we will try our best. Don't worry, I promise you," Anand replied softly as well in Marathi. He was deeply conscious that Shanta had turned down promotions to look after the family over the past few years and now had sacrificed her job entirely to be a trailing wife as his own career took off and he was keen to make every effort to get her the home she desired in Singapore.

Priscilla could not have understood this whispered exchange, but she smiled to herself mysteriously.

As they started to discuss possibilities on the drive home, Priscilla stopped to introduce them to a little shop with a pink-and-white striped awning which she assured them sold the best pizzas and ice creams in Singapore. While the children wolfed down their pizzas as if they had never eaten breakfast, Shanta and Anand discovered through their discussions that with a little personal stretch from their side, they could indeed afford the delightful bungalow.

There was only one hitch.

Priscilla was leaving on Sunday for the US and would be away for several months. And this was a Friday afternoon—leaving them one-and-a-half days only to complete the due diligence and sign the transaction.

Anand was downcast at first, considering this to be a deal-breaker, but relentlessly egged on by Shanta, he made a few calls to senior colleagues whom, to his surprise and delight, he found to be hugely supportive.

A number of people came together for a protracted meeting in the lobby of their hotel on Saturday morning, where diminutive and slow-talking Arthur Ng, legal counsel for Anand's employer, accompanied the Achrekars to review the papers submitted the previous night by Priscilla, which Mr Ng had asked Anand for the previous evening. Mr Ng had brought along one of his juniors and together, they went through all the documents methodically, Priscilla helpfully answering questions and at one stage even going back to her home for a couple of additional documents.

Mr Ng looked at Anand over his half-moon spectacles and asked once, while going through the address proof, "Do you understand the location, Mr Achrekar? Would you want us to go there together once?"

Anand smiled and confirmed that they had already gone through the place together with Priscilla.

Mr Ng nodded thoughtfully, but went back to the documents.

Finally, at the end of almost three hours, as Mr Ng agreed to sign off the agreement, Priscilla heaved a melodramatic sigh of relief and spoke her mind, "Thank goodness—at last! I should be the one going through your documents in more detail since my asset will be under your control!" She uttered, smiling her charismatic smile to take away the sting from her statement.

Mr Ng immediately and courteously offered to provide any additional document she might require, but she waved away his offer good-naturedly. "You are a Government of Singapore company. Once you have signed the lease agreement, I know my home is in the safest of hands," she said. "And with the nicest of families," she continued, turning to put her arm around Shanta, with whom she had struck up a rapport ever since their initial meeting.

Shanta smiled gratefully and hugged Priscilla back warmly as Mr Ng bent his head and signed the agreement; suddenly, the Achrekar family had a new home in Singapore.

❧

Shanta felt a little overwhelmed with the speed at which things had moved, but she was flooded with a glow of contentment that one of the biggest milestones in their move to Singapore had been achieved.

Anand noticed that Shanta could barely contain herself and felt quite good himself. To celebrate the occasion, he invited everyone around the table to lunch at the hotel coffee shop. Mr Ng had an appointment and politely excused himself, but everyone else joined in for a quick soup and sandwich meal. Both Priscilla and Mr Ng's junior lawyer were keen to tell wonderful stories of life in Singapore, so the food was accompanied by lively chatter and a building sense of anticipation on the part of the Achrekars.

After lunch, Priscilla offered to drive them to the house and hand over the keys to all the rooms. Shanta was very keen to get possession so that she could start setting up things as she wanted them and Anand agreed, although he was still a bit concerned that they did not have their own car arranged. However, both Priscilla and Mr Ng's junior reassured him that public transport and safety were two of Singapore's renowned virtues, so he went along.

Shanta took Priscilla aside briefly to request whether they could also take a couple of the trunks that had come with them from Mumbai; these were filled with kitchenware that she wanted to set up as soon as possible. And a suitcase of clothes. The rest would stay on in the hotel until they were completely ready to check out of the hotel and move into their new place.

"Of course, my dear. My Range Rover is as large as it is ancient and it has a big heart, it can carry far more than this," Priscilla responded, grasping Shanta's arm affectionately. "And the sooner you settle in, the sooner the house becomes a home!"

They loaded up with the help of their old friend, the bellboy, and set off, going through what looked like a different route than the one they had taken the previous day, but again through a combination of main roads and side streets.

Once they reached the house, it was a busy time. They unloaded the trunks and carried them into the house, Priscilla proving surprisingly strong and carrying one side herself, while Anand and Shanta together struggled with the other side, which left Anand slightly sulky. After that,

Priscilla took them through each room, handing over keys to the rooms, the bathrooms, the wardrobes, drawers, external doors and gates.

As Anand was signing off the receipts for the various keys, the children helped Shanta drag the trunks into the kitchen, putting newspaper under the edges so they did not scratch the lovely hardwood flooring. Once she unlocked the trunks, Shanta shooed the children away and asked them to unpack their clothes from the suitcases while she set up the kitchen.

As the children clattered away noisily, Shanta plugged in her laptop behind the refrigerator and switched on her favourite music to help her work, tying the dupatta of her salwar kameez around her waist to get started in right earnest.

Priscilla smiled as she saw the excited children emerge into the hallway. "How about some more of that pizza and ice cream?" She offered.

"Oh yes, yes, Priscilla auntie, thank you!" Both Advait and Vaidehi said, jumping up and down excitedly. "Papa, please, please can we go?"

Anand was a bit reluctant to leave Shanta alone to settle in and did not want to have Priscilla do more favours by driving them around. "We really can't keep asking Priscilla to drive us around all the time," he began.

Priscilla noticed his discomfiture and jumped in, "It is just a few minutes away, it will keep them occupied and besides, it has been some time since lunch. I can drop you there and you can take a cab back—your first cab ride to your new home. And you could get a bite back for Shanta, who is already working hard," she added.

This overcame Anand's weak resistance and they all set off in the ancient Range Rover once again.

Anand put up his hand as if asking Priscilla to stop as they joined the traffic on the main road; he was on his phone, trying to call Shanta but could not get a ring. "I need to tell Shanta where we are."

"Don't worry," Priscilla said. "Sometimes the signal drops for a few minutes. Why don't you send Shanta an SMS or a WhatsApp message to update her? The message will go as soon as your phone picks up the signal."

While Anand was typing the message in, they reached their destination and Priscilla dropped them off with goodbyes at the shop with the candy-striped awning, promising to call Shanta to say goodbye to her before she travelled.

Advait and Vaidehi seemed inexplicably hungry again and wolfed down their ten-inch pizzas with gusto, while Anand munched more slowly through his chicken sandwich and tried to call Shanta again—without luck. He was a bit worried that she would not be happy with so much of pizza and ice cream for the children, so as a peace offering, they got a grilled cheese and salad sandwich packed for her before they stepped out and hailed a cab.

The Chinese cab driver was an older, wrinkled man with a flowery shirt worn over shorts and a stylish fedora pulled down over one eye. He puzzled over the address for a moment and then turned to his guidebook. Failing to find it there, he finally turned back to Anand and asked, "Have you got a Google Map location, Mistuh? Canno' find."

Anand was confident that he could guide the cabbie back to their home, since it was not too far. He provided directions while the cabbie drove and within a few minutes, they were at the high wall of the garden next to their home.

"There will be a small right up ahead," Anand said, to keep the driver warned of the little private road in advance.

"There no righ' neah here, suh," grunted the cabbie.

Anand rolled his eyes in the backseat at the cab driver's condescending attitude and said patiently, "It is coming up, please keep an eye out for it."

But as the Toyota moved sedately on past the wall of the private property with beautiful green shrubbery and verdant trees showing over the pristine whitewashed wall, there was no sign of a private road or even of any turning. The more they drove along, the less confident Anand became, twisting in his seat and looking back over the way they had come—maybe they had missed it? Or maybe his directions were wrong?

They reached the end of the wall and stopped at an intersection. The cabbie looked back at Anand and asked, "Where you wan' I turn now, Mistuh?"

Anand asked him to turn around and drive more slowly past the wall, feeling a rising sense of discomfort at Shanta being alone in a house which he could not find. He dialled Shanta again on his mobile phone to ask her to come out on to the main road to flag down the taxi; his anxiety deepened further as he continued to get an out-of-range message.

Shanta had been sorting utensils and vessels from her trunks for almost an hour when she was startled by a sudden pinging sound. As she turned around to look for the source of it, she realised that she was getting a call on Google Duo on her laptop from Priscilla.

She reached out and tapped the answering button, surprised that her laptop seemed to have caught the Wi-Fi without a password.

"Hi Shanta," Priscilla said from the screen. "Sorry, I had to leave, I thought I will call you now."

Shanta smiled and shared her happiness with the kitchen, asking a few questions about the location of the geyser switches and the controls for the cooker oven, which Priscilla answered with enthusiasm.

"Good to see you settling in. You guys are just what this place needed, you know," Priscilla confided in her low, husky voice, making Shanta smile with pride at her little family. "This house has a bit of a history," Priscilla continued. "I don't know whether you would be interested in it?"

"Yes, of course!" Shanta responded enthusiastically, drawing up a chair and opening a bottle of flavoured water.

Priscilla launched into her narrative.

"The bustling, modern human habitat of Singapore was not always like this, you know," she began. "Even today, Singapore is almost 50 per cent green. Most of it is parks and curated greenery, to be sure, but there are rich rolling woodlands too. But a century ago, most of Singapore, or Temasek Island, as it was better known then, was almost fully forested, except for a burgeoning British trading port, which had been set up by Sir Stamford Raffles a century prior and had since continuously showed signs of growth.

"Soon after the First World War, there was a push to grow the trading outpost into a larger settlement. The first order of priority was to get the labour in—those were the long-ago days with limited construction equipment and technology, remember, so most of the work was done by skilled and unskilled Asian labour under the supervision of European architects and engineers."

Shanta recalled that Anand's project was centred around the reconstruction of the old coolie quarters, but she was mindful of his strictures about confidentiality and did not mention it to Priscilla, who was in full flow.

"So it was that a Danish engineer named Anders Johanssen came to Singapore to oversee the building of the coolie quarters. He came over for a visit by himself first, but he was keen to also bring his family of three children and newly pregnant wife since the assignment was to be for at least three years, so he was assigned spacious living quarters in the European cantonment area. However, he was very keen to live closer to his area of operations and looking around, he chanced upon a half-constructed bungalow in a green area which was not too far from the proposed construction site.

"The owners were unknown, so the British government conscripted it and Anders's first mini-construction project was to get the bungalow completed—which is the beautiful house that you are in now."

"Oh, what a lovely story," exclaimed Shanta.

"It is just starting, my dear," Priscilla said, gazing intently at Shanta with unblinking hazel eyes. "Don't you want to hear the rest?"

"Of course, of course," agreed Shanta readily, putting up her feet and settling down more comfortably in her chair.

"It took a few months to get the full team together, during which time the Johanssen family arrived and settled happily into the bungalow. Once all his resources were in place, Anders's first order of work was to define the forest space to be cleared to make way for the construction.

"All his men were of the mind that the forest needed to be cleared by hand, chopping down one tree at a time and digging up the earth manually, but this was going to be time-consuming. Anders was keen to get a head start swiftly and show his superiors he meant business and he was also a great fan of the new explosives used in mining and quarrying, so he overruled all opposition and set out a plan to clear out a three square kilometre patch of forest through a ring of explosives.

"While placing the explosives, a few of his men came back frightened—they reported seeing wild and ferocious beasts glaring at them from the undergrowth. Whispers went around the campfires at night that the spirits of the forest were upset at the intrusion and did not want explosives to rip out their heart. In truth, no one actually came face-to-face with any of the beasts and there were no bloody encounters despite all the anticipation in the camps.

"Nevertheless, the fear remained. A couple of local labourers deserted them and ran away, which Anders duly reported to the Singapore police, indignant that primitive superstition should in any way hold up the project.

"The day of the clearing blasts came soon. Anders had requested the newly appointed British governor, Sir Laurence Guillemard, to push the plunger which set off the chain of explosions that rolled around the interior of the forest, tumbling trees small and large and uprooting all the bushes, leaving the land flattened, with most of the topsoil gone.

"As Anders and Sir Laurence rode around the flattened portions, they were attracted by a sudden commotion amongst the men a half-kilometre away. Riding closer, they found the labourers in various stages of fear and supplication, looking down at three little mangled feline bodies ripped apart by the blasts.

"Lion cubs, was the whispered news to the Europeans as they rode up. 'Nonsense!' Anders replied robustly. 'Everyone knows there are no lions here, it is a myth. These are just cats, who got caught up unfortunately.' Anders waved his supervisors over and pushed them to disperse the gathered men quickly, to get them back to work.

"Sir Laurence looked at Anders quietly for a long moment as they rode on. 'I say, Anders, old chap. If you don't mind my saying so, don't dismiss the labourers so easily, you know. They are the sons of this soil, they know a lot that we will never know. I have seen stranger things than I can care to explain in my stint in India and I have learnt to go slow at times.'

"Anders smiled politely and did not debate the issue further with the governor. But as the day wore into night and the sun rose the next morning, his crew were put back to work with full force.

"Whether it was the pressure of the work, the long hours or anything else, his team and his family noticed a gradual change come over Anders over the next two weeks. He seemed to sleep less, stopped tending to his hitherto well-trimmed muttonchop moustaches and grew increasingly quieter, almost brooding. He was a large, muscular man, but he seemed to shrink a little into himself every day. Despite their whole-hearted inclusion in the outgoing European community in Singapore, he became increasingly reluctant to step out of their home socially and at the end of two weeks, he was almost completely housebound.

"Then came the event that shocked Singapore society and almost stopped the development of the city. The household servants were roused at dawn by high-pitched screams of unmitigated terror from the master bedroom. They rushed there to find an absolutely horrific scene—the children in their nightclothes, huddled into a corner, terrified and shrieking and trembling desperately with fear, staring at Anders who sat on his haunches with empty eyes holding his wife's arm, ripped off at the shoulder, while the rest of her body lay in blood-soaked, shredded pieces all over the room. In a queer little twist, he had a bloody row of safety pins pinned to his arm."

Shanta drew in a sharp breath and slowly uncurled her legs to sit upright, her lustrous eyes widening. But Priscilla continued without a pause.

"The governor was decisive and the police swung into swift action. The children were put in charge of female officers who accompanied them back to Norway on the next ship to their next of kin. The house was cleaned up and put on the market, where it stayed for almost a year before it was bought by a Malaysian businessman of Indian origin, who never used it. Another engineer was rerouted from the Railways in India, a dour Scotsman who had no qualms about taking over the ill-fated project. And in a quiet courtroom trial, a British judge sentenced Anders to an immediate death by hanging, which punishment was carried out within a fortnight.

"Anders pleaded innocence from the time the servants came in, to the police interrogation, through the trial and right up to the moment he was hanged. But his tale was so outlandish and bizarre, it was deemed the outpourings of a deranged mind and disregarded accordingly."

Priscilla stopped for a long moment.

"What…what did he say?" Shanta stammered softly, sitting bolt upright now.

"Anders spoke of a recurring nightmare which he had. The details were crisp and the narrative was fluent—yet it was impossible," began Priscilla.

"Apparently, the night of the clearing blast, Anders had a disquieting dream where he rose in the middle of the night and went to the terrace outside the bedroom and looked out to the edge of the forest in the distance. He saw a majestic lion emerge from the dark heart of the forest, followed by three powerful lionesses. The lion stared silently at him over the distance and Anders swore that he saw the wrath of vengeance in the lion's tawny eyes. He woke out of his fear and found himself standing on his terrace bathed in sweat—but in the distance were only the buildings of Singapore, no forest. And there was no lion.

"The next night, the dream recurred, except that the lion was padding closer, with his lionesses at his heel. And the next night and the next, with the lion getting ever closer. There was a feral smell of the wild which got stronger in Ander's nostrils every night as the lions got closer. Each night Anders forced himself to awaken, finding himself on his terrace, sleeping less and less.

"At the end of a fortnight, the lion had reached the base of the bungalow, with a full moon lighting up his giant maned head as he glared balefully up at Anders, who was filled with a bottomless dread from which he tried to awake with all his might. Once again he found himself on his terrace, but this time he had soiled his nightclothes in his very real terror.

"The whole of the next day and night, Anders tried desperately not to sleep. He tried to convey his fear to his wife, but he could not get a few words out before he realised how crazy he sounded. He drank coffee, he pinched himself, he tied himself upright to his bedside chair, he even pierced his arm with all his wife's safety pins to stay awake. Finally, just before dawn as his eyes closed in slumber despite himself after a fortnight's accumulated sleep deprivation, he found himself in a dream on the terrace overlooking the grounds—but there were no lions there.

"He knew instantly the lions were inside the house! He slapped his wife awake and ran screaming to his children's room in his dream, waking them roughly and dragging them willy-nilly out of the house. As he stumbled and almost fell out of the front door with his children, he looked back up at the house. To his horror, he saw his wife standing alone on the terrace, her eyes filled with sadness in the bright moonlight as she looked down at him.

"He knew immediately that she was sacrificing herself so that her family might be safe and he was completely overcome with grief and guilt. As he dropped his children's hands and shouted out madly to her, she was jerked out of sight like a rag doll by some terrible unseen force. And he awakened to find her blood-spattered, gory remains strewn around their bedroom."

❧

Anand was now beside himself with worry.

He had forced the cabbie to drive around for another ten minutes to no avail. He could not even connect with Shanta on her mobile phone. His increasing aggressive and desperate remarks offended the old cab driver, but the wise Chinaman had seen a lot of visitors in different stages of life and he realised Anand was genuinely worried, so instead of confronting Anand, he offered to call up a police patrol car for help.

The children's incessant prattle dried up as they saw their father fall into panic. They huddled together in a corner of the car and stared at him with wide eyes, intimidated by his highly unusual behaviour.

They drew curious looks from passing cars as they were stopped along the main road bordered by the white-walled garden with Anand striding nervously around the taxicab, still trying Shanta's phone.

As a Singapore Police Fast Response car pulled up, Anand rushed up to the driver's window and started to explain his concerns, his words tumbling over themselves in his nervous hurry. The two smart young policemen got down and asked him a few questions about the location and how they had gotten there earlier, asking the cabbie a few questions too.

Then they waved Anand into the police car.

"My children!" Anand exclaimed, turning to point at the backseat of the cab.

The police waved them in too and then set off, with the taxi closely following.

They followed the white perimeter wall of the garden closely and Anand pointed out where he thought he remembered the private road turning off. The police car reversed and drove past the point slowly again. The two young policemen had a quick conversation in Mandarin and then told Anand briefly, "We go in to find out."

Relieved at some positive action being taken, Anand responded with renewed hope, "Yes, yes. Good idea, I should have thought of that. Whose estate is this? Is it a public garden?"

One of the policemen responded, his answer strangling Anand's newfound hope and squeezing his heart until he could not breathe.

"It is not a garden, Mistah Anan'. This is the Old Singapore Cemetery, from the colonial days," said the young man.

Anand reached out with cold and trembling hands and drew Advait and Vaidehi close to him as the police car turned the corner at the intersection and drove in through a massive wrought iron gate, with an inscription on the wall declaring it to be the Old Singapore Cemetery. The cab driver continued to follow closely. The children were now deeply scared, quiet and tearful, clinging to Anand.

The sun was starting to hang low in the sky by this time, sending long shadows of time-worn tombstones and crosses chasing across the beautifully manicured greenery and paved roadways. The peaceful scene did nothing to quieten the manic pounding of Anand's heart as it thudded against his chest.

The two cars wove their way through the cobbled paths, edging closer to the perimeter wall. They stopped at last and one of the young policemen got out and pointed.

Anand followed his pointing finger to look at a ruined and dilapidated old bungalow, standing next to a much larger flat-roofed, oblong building with three floors and a more commercial exterior, which was well maintained and marked as the Wang family crypt.

The decrepit old bungalow had the faded memory of a once red-tinted roof and gables.

Anand stared in petrified disbelief, shaking in every limb.

He got out of the white police car and tried to walk, but his knees crumbled under him and he fell on the cobbled pathway. He turned to the policeman and cried out in rising, terrible anguish, "What is this place? What is it?! Where is my wife?"

Shanta stared at the screen as Priscilla ended her tale, her mouth slightly open, her breath coming in shallow bursts.

"Why…how… why did you not tell us earlier?" She managed to utter.

"Come on, my dear," Priscilla said cheerfully. "It happened a hundred years ago and was just an interesting tale. Don't let it change what the house means for your family."

Shanta knew in the logical part of her brain that Priscilla made sense, but she was deeply unsettled. She needed to go hug Anand and have him tell her it was all right.

"Yes, well… thank you, I guess," she mumbled, clearly not very keen to continue the conversation.

Priscilla's good mood remained undiminished. "All right then, welcome again to the new house and happy settling in… I will see you again soon." She waved cheerfully and clicked off as Shanta raised a limp hand in response.

Shanta sat for a moment and felt the silence of the house envelop her in a cloying embrace, which she suddenly hated. The sun hung low on the horizon as shadows deepened outside the window, prefacing the sudden dusk of tropical climes.

"Anand?" She called out.

"*Where is my wife*?" She thought she heard Anand call out softly.

Then she heard something heavy being dragged in the master bedroom above the kitchen and realised he must already be moving things around. She put down her flavoured water and got out of her chair quickly and went to the stairs, wrinkling her nose at a sudden feral smell which invaded her senses.

"Anand?" Shanta called again as she started to climb the stairs, unmindful of the dreadful dark shadow which padded behind her.

4

Divine Intervention

When the day dawned, crisp and bright, both Akass and Ajay knew this day was going to change their lives forever.

They were both right, of course.

And they were both so wrong.

The few people in line at the Mother Dairy milk booth looked up at the commotion and most of them smiled at the sight.

A tall, lean young man was attempting to jog down the street but was only managing a series of awkward hops and skips like someone who has just discovered a beetle in his underwear as he tried not to trip over the leashes of the two excited and noisy golden retrievers who were trying to simultaneously show him where to go and circle around him.

Ajay had determinedly set out early on his morning run today as both the important women in his life had decreed that he should undertake important activities today for their peace of mind—and Ajay, good-natured and amiable as he was—had readily agreed.

As usual, his next-door neighbour, the rotund, bespectacled and cheerful Mr Sanyal, had been waiting at his gate to hand over the leash for his two golden retrievers, who were rearing to perform their morning ablutions. Ajay knew that Sanyal Babu had been strictly instructed by Mrs Sanyal to take the dogs out for a walk every morning in order to ensure the portly old lawyer got his daily dose of exercise, but Mr Sanyal had outwitted her by cleverly reaching an outsourcing arrangement with his energetic and willing neighbour. Thus, it fell upon Ajay to gallivant with energetic canines every morning while Sanyal Babu himself spent a relaxing hour in his Jaguar with the air-conditioning switched on, WhatsApping with his lawyer friends and eating some deep-fried, forbidden breakfast sneakily delivered by Swiggy.

It always brought a smile to Ajay's face to think of Mr Sanyal's unique approach. A more stringent critic may have thought it necessary to admonish Mr Sanyal and lecture him on his responsibilities towards his health; or a craven might have even contemplated an anonymous tip to the redoubtable Mrs Sanyal (anonymous because only someone with a death wish would risk a face-to-face encounter with a Bengali lady with lung power, generous vocabulary and volatile temperament like Mr Sanyal's life partner...). But Ajay had a much more relaxed and liberal view of life than that, he genuinely believed in live and let live; besides, he knew Mr Sanyal from childhood and he felt that such a successful legal mind could be trusted not to be short-sighted about his own health.

An hour later, he was towelling off his head after a shower as his old faithful retainer Ramdass brought him his morning poha and coffee. Ramdass had started working for his parents when they got married and had stayed on ever since, through their three children and two of his own. He cared deeply about Ajay as the youngest of the Kapoor children, but it was an open secret that he was the senior Mrs Kapoor's eyes and ears in Ajay's life. Ajay knew that very well too, but as with everything else, his affection for both his mother and for Ramdass overcame any objections he might have felt.

He chewed the poha ruminatively, wishing Ramdass would heed his instructions and serve him up the scrambled eggs he wanted in the morning. But it seemed to be Ramdass's mission in life to make as much of Ajay's diet vegetarian as possible. He grinned as he imagined Ramdass getting "Vegetarianism for Ajay" as one of his annual performance objectives from his mother.

Mrs Radha Kapoor was a petite, energetic lady who was fiercely protective of her family despite their well-demonstrated capability to look after themselves. She had married Ajay's father, then a mere aspiring chartered accountant, four decades ago in a marriage arranged by their families. They had seen some very tough years financially and then slow and steady success—not unlike millions of other couples of that generation in India who lived through economic liberalisation and its benefits.

Ajay was her youngest offspring and unashamedly her favourite, a child of their success, who had never seen the tough times they had lived through. He was raised in privilege, yet he was the one who had the most empathy and consideration for others, which made her love him all the more.

When Ajay was born, almost three decades ago, his grandparents had been a little startled and his parents a little embarrassed—almost as if it had been assumed by the wider family that they had turned celibate after their second child eleven years before. Ajay's infancy had slowly turned into a battleground for grandparent supremacy, much to his benefit and the chagrin of his elder siblings.

Radha Kapoor's father had retired from his senior government job by that time and was dabbling in day trading, so he decided to stop gifting his grandchildren gold coins as commemorative items and chose to gift the blissfully ignorant Ajay a thousand shares in the IPO of an up and coming IT firm called Infosys on his first birthday. Ajay's paternal grandfather, a very competitive small business owner, had gritted his teeth at thus being outdone and had nursed the wound, since he fancied himself more of a cosmopolitan citizen of the world. But he found the perfect opportunity at last and presented Ajay on his fourth birthday with two thousand dollars of US shares in the IPO of a book delivery platform called Amazon.

All of which meant that Ajay was a full-fledged multimillionaire by the time he was a teenager, even though he got the right to use the money only when he was twenty-one.

"Memsaab had called while you were out playing. Three times. But you were not here," said Ramdass, seeming slightly offended that Mrs Kapoor had been thus denied.

As if on cue, Ajay's mobile rang. It was his mother.

"Beta, where were you? Ramdass was so worried, he did not know your whereabouts," she started.

Before he could reassure her that he had only been doing what he did every morning, she continued, "You know that today is very important, I have got the entire family coming, so at last your ugly, boxy car will come in useful. Please be at our gate at eleven, I have assigned three of your aunts to travel with you."

"Of course, I know Ma, I will be there…" he started to confirm, but she was off again.

"These prayers are for Mausaji, but our whole prayer meeting is also important for Binu Mausi. We need to strengthen her at this difficult time. Please wear the special shoes Mausaji made for you. Your Papa is refusing to wear them, he wants to wear his open-toed chappals. He is always claiming he has gout, but no, we must still have kebabs every day. And single malt is consumed like nimbu pani in this house—"

"What about Bhaiya, why can't he wear his pair?" Ajay broke in, reluctant to risk the handmade, custom-fitted wine-coloured brogues in a temple where he was highly concerned they would be stealthily pilfered by some greedy, amoral temple-goer with feet the same size.

Apparently, that was a touchy topic with Mrs Radha Kapoor, who spent another few minutes bemoaning that she had raised a criminally venal elder son who was not sensitive enough to shut down his entire office and cancel all client meetings when his mother called for a prayer meeting at short notice. Ajay could not help but grin at this flagrantly unfair description of his hardworking brother, a highly respected partner at KPMG, but he knew better than to try and defend him.

Ajay had felt a brooding uneasiness about his mother's planned outing ever since she had sprung the plan on her unsuspecting family. It was not just his natural aversion to temples—although he could never fully forget the startling horror of letting go of his mother's hand in a temple when he was two years old and finding himself suddenly adrift in a sea of what appeared to be a veritable sea of unwashed feet—it was just that he had never seen anything other than chaos when two or more of his aunts got together, especially in public places which seemed to encourage them to freely express their choicest eccentricities.

He was not irreligious, but he was a bit sceptical whether a large crowd of his aunts mobbing the neighbourhood temple could inveigle the Almighty into bringing his ailing Mausaji out of his coma. The adventurous old gentleman had completed nine decades, being two decades older than Binu Mausi, and these years had been richly lived to the fullest with celebration, travel, success, food and drink and, if Ajay knew him, probably several banned substances too. Mausaji had accomplished all that he had been keen to and had in fact been making it clear for a few years now that he now wanted to pass away peacefully when his time came.

Nevertheless, Ajay recognised the expedition was important for his Mausi and his mother's peace of mind and he dutifully dressed in his best, down to the wine-coloured handmade brogues that Mausaji had gifted him last year. The crusty old tycoon had transformed the family shop of Chadha's Chappals into a massive luxury leather conglomerate, but he was proudest of the handmade shoes that were so exclusive and sought after that they could cost as much as a small new car.

Despite Ajay's grim foreboding, the actual outing itself took no more than a couple of hours and went off without any major disaster—although his eldest aunt pottered off into the lane next to the temple and was missing for half an hour before she was rescued by a kindly tea stall owner; another aunt had to be forcibly restrained from handing over the entire contents of her purse to a densely bearded charlatan who claimed to have the cure for heart attacks. Even his father's long-suffering growling did not deter his bevy of aunts, who assailed the Almighty in various tones of pious prayer for almost an hour.

Ajay had dutifully followed the prayers with the rest and tried hard to focus on the rituals, but as his family procession began to straggle out of the temple and started thronging the shoe counter outside, his thoughts turned to the next challenge awaiting him today.

Major General Mervyn Charles Fernandes, retired.

Jennifer had relentlessly painted the picture of a larger than life man, a career soldier from a family of career soldiers (which Ajay irreverently thought seemed to show a lack of independent thinking). General Fernandes apparently espoused a number of values which were politely referred to as 'old-fashioned', a collective description of a value system that was mired in his memories of his youth—which must have been in some ancient prehistoric time, or so it seemed to Ajay.

Ajay was all for gallantry and duty and integrity, of course, but he was not sure what he should do about "being a man's man". Other than anything else, he was extremely wary of being "masterful around women", especially his beloved Jennifer, whose expression of cold anger could quell a nascent rebellion more effectively and ruthlessly than any General he had ever heard of.

The general, together with his gentle wife Sylvia, seemed to have been a highly competitive baby-maker in his youth, being responsible for five robust children. Much to his consternation, the first three had been girls, leaving him confounded about how he could further the family military lineage. However, the following two boys were of great solace to him and he immersed himself in their upbringing and watched with beaming pride as they too joined the army when their time came.

His daughters the general loved completely and joyfully. He enjoyed basking in their affectionate attention, but he discovered early in their lives that their habits, thoughts and demands were quite alien to him. He was baffled when he was asked to turn vegetarian to prevent further cruelty to animals; or when his interpretation of casual clothing entailed an ensemble of crisply pressed trousers with cravat and tweed jacket and was aggressively challenged; or even when he was asked to be more soft-spoken with his batman. He was quite content to leave their secrets and their teenage emotions to his gentle Sylvia, although he was fiercely protective of them and almost never missed any special occasion in their lives—be it birthdays, school plays, graduation or the day his eldest became a doctor or her sister took up teaching or when Jennifer graduated in law from Columbia University.

The very thought of being scrutinised by this redoubtable man brought a twinge of pain in Ajay's legs as they all headed out from the temple. He idly wondered if he had caught some foul bug on the temple floor as they waited for their cavalcade of cars.

"Are you off to meet that general chap?" his father asked.

As Ajay nodded, his father muttered grouchily, "Why does he get to do all the approvals? Why shouldn't I get to approve Jennifer?"

"Don't be silly!" Radha Kapoor admonished him. "You have known Jennifer since she and Ajay were going out in the US and you know you adore her!"

"Of course, I like her a lot and I don't understand at all why she wants to marry this unemployed duffer son of ours," Ajay's father conceded, backing down but still grouchy after the temple experience with all his wife's sisters and cousins, "it's just that it isn't fair that this general chap gets to approve and I don't."

Ajay wanted to ask his father for some serious last-minute advice (Mr Kapoor had cheerfully told him the previous night to boldly deny any accusations, which worried Ajay as it seemed his father viewed him as some sort of fugitive from justice) but he had to turn his attention to bundling various aunts into his Audi Q7, which proved to be a bit of a task since they were trying to climb into the high car head-first, resulting in embarrassing displays of their nether regions to several jobless youth who had appeared from nowhere to pass thoughtfully offensive remarks.

As he sat next to the driver dropping them off to their homes, the twinge of pain in his legs came back a little more strongly. "I should not have run this morning," he thought ruefully, his nervousness becoming a bit more pronounced.

After dropping them all off, he was relieved to find that he had more than enough time to make his way to the hotel in Connaught Place, although the pain in his legs had intensified a bit. He winced as he hopped down from the car and walked gingerly into the lobby and looked around. Apart from the staff and two burly Caucasian males adorned in shorts, t-shirts and colourful tattoos, the other guests were all women, so he took a seat and stared apprehensively at the entrance.

General Fernandes appeared briskly within a few minutes, early as well, determined to try and catch the Ajay fellow on the wrong foot if possible. It was impossible to mistake him for anything other than a senior armed forces officer, with his neatly parted short grey hair, the crisply pressed suit with the knife-edge crease in his trousers and the resplendent bristly moustache that seemed to enter the room before him.

Ajay jumped up and trotted over to him, forgetting the pain in his legs for a moment. "General Fernandes?" he asked.

The General stood ramrod straight and looked him over. "Are you Ajit?"

"Erm…actually…" stammered Ajay, confused whether he had the wrong person or whether the general was genuinely incapable of remembering one of the shortest names in India.

"Eh? Speak up, man," barked the general, enjoying himself.

The pain in his legs came back in a wave suddenly and it was so much more intense than earlier that it overcame Ajay's sense of propriety. "I asked you first!" He said tersely. "Surely courtesy demands you respond first?"

A grudging light of respect dawned in the general's narrowed eyes. *Tough*, he thought to himself, because a man's man thought in monosyllables, without babbling like a girl.

Aloud, he cleared his throat ostentatiously and said, "Yes indeed, I am General Fernandes."

Ajay remembered himself and smiled, proffering his hand. "A pleasure to meet you, sir, I am Ajay Kapoor."

As he took a step forward to shake the general's hand, there was another shooting pain in his right leg and as he suppressed his yelp of pain, his hand pressed down hard on the general's.

The old soldier was encouraged to find his hand engulfed in an iron grip and he took up the challenge with a gusto born of a lifetime of overcoming physical challenges. The two men remained with their hands locked in a long moment which threatened to become an unseemly period of time, while smiling fiercely at each other.

What the hell? Ajay thought.

Manly, thought the general in another monosyllable.

After they disentangled themselves from their little unintended contest, they made their way to the multicuisine restaurant where Jennifer had already booked them a table. On the way, Ajay made a couple of well-thought-through and highly researched comments about the weather, including some erudite insights on global warming which he had memorised. However, he surmised correctly from the general's noncommittal grunts that he cared so little about discussing the weather that he would not even express it in words.

Ajay was offered a brief respite from the burden of having to converse by a bubbly young hostess, who prattled cheerfully as she seated them and took their drinks orders.

The general unhesitatingly ordered a scotch on the rocks without consulting the menu and turned to watch Ajay keenly, who he strongly suspected of being a namby-pamby wine drinker, no doubt fitting only to be seated with the memsaabs during the battalion parties.

Ajay would normally have had a pleasant and knowledgeable discussion on the merits of the different wines on the wine list, but today, he quickly needed something strong to help deaden the pain in his legs. "Scotch for me as well. Single malt. Make it a double," he said.

Another thought struck him, learnt during a leisurely whiskey tour in Scotland. "None of that twelve-year stuff, I want the choice eighteen-year-old please."

The general admittedly felt some relief, but he was a tough old warrior and was not yet satisfied. He continued to watch Ajay like a hawk as he picked up the food menu. If Ajay was going to argue about the relative merits of different salads or order a fish, the general felt he would be justified in continuing to have concerns.

But Ajay was in no mood to waste time on the menu. He opened it and ordered the first thing that met his eye. "Roast mutton with mint sauce."

General Fernandes's shoulders relaxed slightly and he leaned back.

After a few desultory observations on their surroundings, the drinks arrived. As Ajay asked for a repeat and proceeded to gulp his whiskey down, the general felt it was time to address the elephant in the room.

"Ahem!" He harrumphed. "What do you think of religion?"

Ajay had been brooding on the cause of his pain and he was feeling more and more certain some horrible disease had attacked his bare feet in the temple, which had, of course, also been filled with other people's bare feet no doubt carrying a vile plethora of germs. So it was with a clear conscience that he replied simply, "I see absolutely no need to visit temples.

"Or mosques…" he added, as he remembered that shoes had to be taken off before prayers in their neighbourhood mosque. "I am not so sure about churches…." He ended, with a crinkled brow as he tried to remember whether he had ever seen a pile of shoes outside a church.

There was some excitable movement in the bushy moustache as General Fernandes breathed in sharply. The second round of drinks arrived and prevented him from expressing his approval openly, but mentally he felt that Ajay had reflected the army ethos that faith was personal and all religions were fine as long as the followers were not overcome by blind primitive beliefs and superstitions. He also liked the fact that Ajay, decent chap that he was, had hesitated about churches, in deference to his Christian guest.

Feeling more at ease, he felt the time was ripe to quiz Ajay on his views on modern Indian women.

Ajay had taken a few deep sips of his second double whiskey and was not sure what the question meant, so he asked the general, "Why don't you tell me, sir?"

"Well, I feel damned unhappy about some of the dodgy places that Jennifer visits which I believe may not be safe for her, but she does not seem to understand my concern…" started off the old soldier, meaning the underprivileged areas that his daughter spent time in as part of her work in her NGO, where he was worried she might catch a disease or be too exposed to the tragic underbelly of city life.

"Yes, exactly, I could not agree more!" Ajay exclaimed, thinking of the times he had wanted to accompany Jennifer in night rescue missions for women and children and she had mistaken his concern for patriarchy.

Thus encouraged, General Fernandes warmed up to his task.

He loved his daughters and he basked in their love of him. But there was no gainsaying that he understood them in little bits and pieces and most of the time not at all. He never spoke of this to his fellow officers and friends, of course. So as he began speaking, a lifetime of confusion unburdened itself. Why did bedsheets have to have designs, what was wrong with white? Why did every relative for a thousand kilometres around have to be visited? Why did he have to consider his subordinates' feelings when barking orders? Why did he have to wear mauve-coloured shirts—in fact, what kind of a damned colour was mauve? Why did he have to avoid seeing some bloody popular film, which all his friends had seen, because the protagonist was apparently a misogynist—it was just a film?

There was a brief interlude when the food was served and both men attacked their lunch. By then, Ajay was floating on a happy alcohol-induced cloud after his third double whiskey and he encouraged general Fernandes to continue.

From then on, it was practically a love feast. General Fernandes gratefully accepted Ajay's glazed eyes and fixed smile as expressing tacit agreement; the feisty old gentleman felt increasingly lighter as he talked through all those occasions when he had done what his daughters asked out of love for them but he had been consumed with an inner bafflement. By the time the meal ended and they were saying their goodbyes in the domed atrium entrance, they were on the best of terms and the General was practically referring to Ajay as "My boy".

There was one horrible moment of doubt at the end where it seemed that Ajay would be overcome by the situation and consume the general in a warm embrace, but fortunately, another twinge of pain in his legs deterred Ajay and the moment passed safely.

After an alcohol-fuelled, heavy lunch in the afternoon, both of which were unusual for him, Ajay nodded off gently in the car as his driver, another one of Mrs Kapoor's implanted spies, drove him sedately home. He was woken close to home by his mobile phone bursting explosively into life—it was Jennifer.

"Hello? Hello? Baby? Wow, what did you do? Dad loves you and he has totally blessed us! Tell me, what did you do?"

Ajay's senses came sharply back as he straightened up and his legs reminded him immediately that they were in pain.

In his grouchy state, he felt that Jennifer's question was unfair to him. "What do you mean what did I do?" he asked in a querulous tone. "I was me and he must have liked me, why is that surprising?"

"Of course, you are totally lovable, my sweety, you know that. I think you are so cute! But Daddy kept saying you were a man's man and a tough guy—that didn't sound like you, baby," Jennifer explained. "So, tell me what you did? How did you manage it?" She asked again.

Ajay definitely felt miffed now, as the alcohol continued to wear off and the pain started winning.

"I was just me," he said testily. "Maybe the old codger opened his mind at last and saw the steel in me." He thought over his statement as there was a chilly pause at the other end.

"It seems his daughter cannot recognise steel when she sees it," he added, for good measure.

"Are you still playing tough guy?" Jennifer asked in an ominous tone. "Well, I don't like it." She continued, "This is not the Ajay I love and want to live the rest of my life with."

Ajay vaguely felt he should say something reassuring, but they were at his building now and he desperately wanted to go home, change into his pyjamas and jump into bed with a strong painkiller. "Father wants strong, daughter does not—come on, make up your mind!" He growled defensively.

"Oh? Is that so?" The steel in Jennifer's voice was unmistakeable. "Call me back when you are behaving better," she snapped and hung up.

Ajay was already on his way in to the house, looking for pain relief.

At that moment, halfway across the city outside a deserted warehouse on the outskirts of Kamla Nagar, Akass was having a tough time of his own.

Akass was the first of his family to have been born in a big city, in a posh English-speaking hospital arranged by his father's employer. His parents intended to name him Akash Kumar, of course, but the superior attitude of the condescending registrar in the hospital combined with his father's hesitant literacy and rustic pronunciation meant he was forever Akass Kumar.

As he lay face down on the dusty floor listening to Faisal Bhai's heavy footsteps getting closer, he realised in a sudden rush of understanding that this was what his parents had been trying to warn him against.

His father Yogesh Kumar had come to Delhi from Bihar in search of a job and had, by incredible good fortune, found a lifelong mentor and benefactor in his first employer, Dhananjay Chadha. Yogesh Kumar had started as a labourer in the Chadha factory, moved upwards to the factory line and was now comfortably ensconced in a relatively higher-paying job as the trusted family driver, with his elder son now working in the delivery line in the factory.

While the Kumars had graduated over a period of time to cosy quarters in a locality near the main Chadha mansion, young Akass had been exposed from an early age to the lavish lifestyle of the Chadha family and aspired to achieve that quality of life for himself. It was a bit annoying that his father and elder brother kept unnecessarily nagging him about hard work and values and education, overlooking the vital fact that Akass was a highly skilled graduate of the University of WhatsApp and Facebook and was therefore fully aware that there were many shortcuts to wealth—all he had to do was to find the magic key.

Akass's relentless search for a shortcut to wealth had led him to pursue many promising avenues—he had almost been expelled from the nearby government school when he had industriously tried to arm all the students with country-made knives on behalf of a dubious businessman who had mysteriously disappeared when telephoned by the principal of the school; he had willingly provided his mother's meagre gold jewellery to a holy man with an authentic beard and a band of devoted followers who had committed to use the starter gold to turn all the steel and aluminium in their house to gold but who was unfortunately called away on a private family emergency before he could perform the rituals; Akass had even brought home a stock market expert who could have transformed their family's monthly income into millions, but his parents had been unduly suspicious of the expert's frayed clothes and lack of permanent address and they had thus forsaken the opportunity.

But Akass was a resilient soul and he remained determined to find that elusive doorway to immediate wealth, notwithstanding the disappointments that had befallen him along the way. And he felt that the universe had conspired to reward him when his path crossed Jagga's.

Jagga was a phenomenon that suddenly swept the crowded, working class neighbourhood where their friends and relatives lived. From the top of Jagga's improbably blonde head, through his fake Dolce & Gabbana dark glasses, the shiny profusion of doubtful gold necklaces that adorned his scrawny neck, the fake Gucci t-shirts and the fake Yeezees on his feet—he was designed to overwhelm the casual onlooker and maybe even bedazzle those that caught a glimpse of him from the corner of their eyes. He appeared from nowhere, apparently borne by the summer winds, claiming kinship to various neighbours who had since moved away. He seemed to know all sorts of secrets about the rich and the famous (no one fact-checked his stories) and always had money to spend without any apparent sign of employment.

In short, he appeared to be living Akass's dream.

Akass made no bones about his open-mouthed admiration for Jagga and was soon one of Jagga's permanent camp followers—much to the dismay of his parents who were keen that Akass finish school and move on to some respectable employment. But Akass had daydreamed his way through all his classes and failed at the final hurdle several times; while this made him a much respected elder statesman amongst his much younger classmates, it also crystallised his belief that Destiny had something else in mind for him.

So it transpired that when Jagga discovered that Akass could drive a range of international cars (courtesy of his father's employer who kindly allowed him to train on all his cars), Jagga had a discreet conversation with Akass intimating that if he was interested, there could be a wealthy payoff for using these skills in the service of Jagga's own mentor—Faisal Bhai.

"Absolutely not!" Yogesh had said when Akass put the question to him. "You will finish your studies before we discuss anything else."

His mother had more to say. "What sort of a name is Faisal Bhai? What work will you do for him? Your father drives for one of the biggest businessmen in the city—how can you expect to get paid more than that? And what will we tell the neighbours?"

Akass briefly but colourfully described what they should tell the neighbours, which made his father snort. While Yogesh quickly pretended it was the start of a coughing fit and used it as an excuse to leave the room, it was enough to upset Akass's mother and bring down a storm of recriminations on Akass's rebellious head, from which he had to be rescued by his middle brother, who lived with them in the relatively spacious three-room tenement.

A temporary truce was finally arranged by his eldest brother and sister-in-law, who lived next door.

It was agreed that Akass could go with Jagga to meet Faisal Bhai, but only if he spent an hour in pious prayer at the temple with his mother beforehand and reported everything verbatim to his entire family on his return.

So this morning, Akass had carefully dressed in his borrowed best—his eldest brother's original Levi's jeans, surreptitiously smuggled to him by his sister-in-law; his own best shiny gold-coloured satin shirt; new socks purchased for the occasion; and his father's handmade shoes that his employer had gifted him. And faithfully accompanied his mother to the temple, from where the redoubtable Jagga picked him up after what seemed like a week of ringing bells and chanting but was actually a little less than an hour.

He was surprised and vaguely disappointed when Jagga jumped into a waiting Uber. His surprise deepened when they stopped outside a large flat warehouse, clearly deserted and visibly decrepit, which they smelt long before they saw. He felt himself sweating into the valued gold shirt and his feet were slipping inside his father's shoes as if they had suddenly grown a size larger, forcing him to ask Jagga, "Here? What is this place?"

Jagga allowed himself a superior smile at his protégé's naivety. "Wait bubba, you will see," he said in the smug manner of one who was sure of the future.

They waited outside the warehouse in the afternoon sun for some time while Jagga made a few whispered phone calls and Akass's perspiration turned his shirt from shiny to dull gold. Finally, a sleek black BMW 7 Series appeared at the far end of the compound and made its way towards them. As it rolled to a stop, a thin dark fellow who could have been Jagga's long-lost twin leaped out of the driver's door and ceremoniously opened the rear passenger door as an impressive personage stepped out.

While the top of his head was balding, long, red, hennaed fronds curled down the side and back of his head incongruously. He appeared to be wearing an expensive ring on every finger and his huge frame showed a once muscular body gone to fat, encased in an expensive designer suit. From Jagga's suddenly obsequious body language, Akass guessed this must be Faisal Bhai.

Deep-set hazel eyes in a fair-complexioned face looked penetratingly at Akass. "Tho, ith thith the phellow who can drive fatht carth?" Faisal Bhai asked in a deep voice.

At the unexpected lisp, Akass felt a nervous giggle about to burst out of him, but was prevented by Jagga quickly stepping hard on his toe.

"Yes, Bhai," Jagga responded meekly. "He can drive all sorts of expensive foreign cars. His father drives for a rich businessman," he continued by way of explanation. "And Akass is a good boy, he is very keen to work with you."

Faisal Bhai seemed unimpressed with this character certificate from Jagga. He remained lost in thought for a while, after which he spoke directly to Akass.

"In our bidneth, we donth get thecond chanthes. Tho lithen carefully, Akath," he began in a low voice, nonetheless menacing because of the lisp. "Drive thith car towardth the other thide of the warehouthe and then turn tightly and return. Ath you return, one of the doorth will open, but you will not know in advanth which door. You have to turn the car through that door immediately. And you have to drive your fathteth, thow me what you can do!" He commanded.

Akass was keen to ask what the 'bidneth' was, because he was concerned about the apparent paucity of second chances it offered, but he forced himself to focus on the task at hand. Jagga's long-lost twin threw the BMW key case to him as Akass walked towards the car. His feet felt as if they were sliding around in his father's shoes and he wondered wildly for a moment whether his feet had shrunk due to the tension, but all other thoughts were wiped away as he got into the car.

He knew the make and model well and his confidence surged. Switching on the engine, he slipped it into the Sport mode, executed a tight U-turn and held his fingers over the manual gearshifts on the steering wheel as he stepped on the accelerator.

The big car responded to his foot on the accelerator and surged forward with a roar.

And then, inexplicably and to Akass's utter shock, his foot slipped inside his shoe, slid off the accelerator and got stuck under it.

The surge of power ended as quickly as it had begun and the car slowed down suddenly to a roll as Akass struggled to free his foot. As he desperately struggled, his foot surprisingly came clear out of the shoe, leaving the confounded piece of footwear firmly wedged under the accelerator, preventing any further driving. As Akass bent down to pull his shoe out, the steering wheel tilted to one side and the majestic vehicle nudged into the vine-covered filthy wall of the warehouse, dragging along with an offended screeching sound.

Heart pounding and shoe finally in hand, Akass shakily got out of the car to find Faisal Bhai standing uncomfortably close while Jagga and his long-lost twin looked on, their horror-struck expressions boding ill for Akass.

Faisal Bhai appeared to be in the throes of some great emotion which contorted all his features, but after grappling with it for a few seconds, he spoke in a sibilant whisper.

"You &%$@#!" He hissed menacingly, displaying an enormous vocabulary and an impressive knowledge of biology. "Damned @#&$$ %%$@# !@#$%...!" He continued in a rising voice, recklessly assuming all sorts of unspeakable incestuous acts in Akass's immediate family.

"If you did not know how to drive, why did you ekthperiment with my ekthpenthive car, you *&%%$#? You thould be killed for thith!"

"Please, please Faisal Bhai..." Akass dropped to his knees with his hands folded in supplication. "I do know how to drive. I do, I do. But this time, I don't know what happened. My shoes... my shoes..." he spoke wildly. "Please believe me, I am telling the truth, I swear on my parents. Give me a second chance and I will prove myself..." Akass pleaded.

"Thecond thanth? I told you we have no thecond chanthes in our bidneth!" Faisal Bhai growled.

"But you know what? Maybe I will give you another chanth," he continued, reaching a giant hand into his pocket and withdrawing an evil-looking, snub-nosed pistol with a deeply metallic glint. "When the polith find uth, we have to thcatter and run. Thow me how fatht you can ethcape!"

Seeing Akass's face where dumbfounded disbelief was struggling with hysterical fear, Faisal Bhai realised that Akass was dealing with a completely new situation and might need further motivation.

He obligingly raised the gun and fired into the cement floor next to Akass's feet, which splintered in an impressive burst.

Akass scraped his knee badly as he scrambled to his feet with mad urgency and turned to run. He had barely taken a couple of leaping steps when his feet slipped and turned inside his shoes and he tottered forward, comically out of balance with his arms outstretched before tripping and falling flat on his face.

An unpleasant suspicion about Faisal Bhai's 'bidneth' had now crystallised clearly into unwilling realisation in Akass's terrified mind. He realised that Jagga was not a prophet of good times but was actually the village idiot, who had lured him into auditioning for a hardened gangster almost certainly dealing in stolen cars, who it seemed had no compunctions about taking a fellow human being's life willy-nilly. He was horribly confused how he had managed to fail the audition, but he was suddenly surprised to find he was completely glad that he had.

He feverishly realised that he would now never be able to tell his parents that they were right and that he loved them, because now Faisal Bhai was going to kill him.

As he lay face down on the dusty floor listening to Faisal Bhai's heavy footsteps getting closer, he realised in a rush of understanding that this was what his parents had been trying to tell him.

The heavy, deliberate footsteps stopped near him. They were followed by the skittering steps of Jagga and his long-lost twin who came running up.

Akass closed his eyes and began to softly weep, waiting for the bullet to decimate his frightened brain. For a few long moments, there was no sound other than his sniffling. This was followed by mournful hacking, like the cough of an agitated cow.

Akass looked up timidly, to find himself looking at Faisal Bhai displaying a large number of gold teeth, while Jagga and his long-lost twin were also happily displaying dental structures of uncertain colour and hygiene.

"You are a danger to yourthelf, you thad and dithguthting ⋆&@#$," Faisal Bhai managed through his hoarse chuckling, offensive to the last. "Get out of here and never thow me your fathe again!"

❧

The call came in the early hours of the morning.

In the dead of the night, soon after his daughter reached Delhi from her home in Australia, Mausaji had quietly passed away.

Ajay put on a white kurta over his lightest blue jeans and—with moist emotion blurring his vision—he put on Mausaji's gifted shoes to go to see him one last time.

Then he called his parents, picked them up on the way and drove to Binu Mausi's home, not too far away, where the whole family had started to congregate.

There were already a few cars parked outside, and neighbours had also started to visit to offer condolences and pay their respects to the departed, who had been a well-liked and respected man. Ajay looked askance at the mixed pile of shoes at the main entrance lobby and thoughtfully tucked his expensive handmade brogues under the sofa at the back of the pile, so that none of the mourners could trample over it.

Binu Mausi was a warm puddle of emotional tears, but she still wanted to ensure everyone was fed and looked after. Ajay held her close for a long and heartfelt hug and was going to ask her to relax, but his mother signalled him not to. "She needs to do something to postpone the grief, beta. Let her get involved in silly little tasks," was Mrs Kapoor's sage advice.

Ajay was put to work serving innumerable cups of tea to the flow of guests. After what felt like the millionth cup he served, Ajay felt a light touch on his arm and turned to find Jennifer at his elbow.

"I am so sorry, baby," she said in a choked voice. "He was a good man and so kind to you. And to me," she added tearfully.

Ajay enveloped her in a bear hug, just happy to have her presence next to him. He leaned back to look apprehensively at her face as he remembered their argument the previous day, but Jennifer looked steadily back at him and shook her head. "Don't worry about a silly little argument at this time."

He hugged her again in relief. "My feet were paining so badly, it made me so grumpy. I am so sorry, darling."

Jennifer looked at him in concern. "Are your feet still paining? We should go and consult a doctor today. Let me see if I can make an appointment…"

"No, no—don't worry so much," demurred Ajay, who did not like to be fussed over. "It was just yesterday, nothing after that," he said, overlooking the twinges he had felt when driving over this morning.

"Well, whatever your mood was yesterday, it worked on Daddy," said Jennifer, cheerfully focusing on the positive.

Mrs Radha Kapoor had come up and had caught the end of the conversation. She spoke her conviction, "It was divine intervention, beta. We had all gone to the temple in the morning, you see."

"Hanuman Ji spoke to Jesus Christ, did he?" Ajay grinned, but was quelled by identical looks from his mother and his beloved which seemed to indicate he was skating on thin ice.

"Listen, I need you both to go and get fresh samosas and mithai for the guests," Mrs Kapoor said, getting back to her duties. "Mausaji's car and driver are here, please go to his favourite shop in Green Park and buy enough to last us the day, the guests are continuing to pour in now."

As they obediently made their way out, Ajay was momentarily irritated to find his handmade, wine-coloured brogues on top of the pile of shoes. Some annoying busybody must have dug them out from under the sofa.

They put on their shoes and walked out arm in arm into the weak, wintry morning sunshine.

Mausaji's driver Yogesh hurried out of the house after them and stopped short—he could not see the fine handmade shoes his employer Mr Chadha had gifted him where he had left them, on top of the pile of shoes. He searched in increasing frenzy for a few minutes and then, to his intense relief, he discovered them under the sofa at the back.

They had seemed too large for him this morning when he had worn them to pay his last respects to his beloved employer and he had freely blamed his thoughtless son Akass for wearing them the previous day. But as he laced them up now, they seemed to have recovered their perfect fit.

5

Rebellion

The British commissioner of Oudh set down his morning cup of tea with a soft clink and spoke thoughtfully, almost as if he was sifting through his own feelings and dusting them off in the light of day. "There is rebellion in the air, you know, lad."

He sighed and leaned back into the comfortably cushioned cane sofa, pushing back his long, thinning salt-and-pepper hair with the calloused fingers of a military man who has seen a lot of service. "I am an old hand at this, I can smell it…" he continued reflectively.

They were in the most peaceful of early morning settings, on the veranda of the British residency in Lucknow, on a sun-dappled day in March 1857, facing a large pristine green meadow surrounded by apple and oak trees, with the chirping and calls of a myriad Indian birds to keep them company.

All the while, a crisply turbaned *khansama* kept a vigilant eye on the two footmen serving breakfast to the sahibs.

Since the brigadier had assumed charge of his responsibilities in Lucknow a couple of months ago, he had done a tremendous amount to try and repair the damage his predecessor had wrought with his intemperate actions. So Richard was unsure whether Sir Henry's pessimism was a feeble attempt at self-deprecating humour or whether he had been momentarily overcome by something terrible which had happened to him recently.

From what he had seen of the politically savvy old soldier, neither pessimism nor humility was a part of his gruff, no nonsense mental make-up.

With his weather-beaten blue eyes twinkling above his grizzled salt-and-pepper beard, Brigadier General Sir Henry Montgomery Lawrence resembled nothing so much as an overgrown, mischievous leprechaun, thought the Right Honourable Richard Lytton-Whyte sitting opposite him. This made it even more difficult to take the old soldier's seemingly portentous observation seriously.

Richard tilted his head in a polite gesture and smiled questioningly at his superior officer.

Sir Henry caught the smile and grunted, "Aye lad, beats me too. Heaven knows we are doing a lot for these godless natives; the educated few who understand or speak a bit of our civilised language are soon thankful enough. But the great unwashed mass of these Indians don't even recognise what is good for them, that's really the core of the problem. British civilisation is bringing them far greater administrative efficiency and a much stronger law and order machinery courtesy of the East India Company, but they just do not seem to understand..."

Sir Henry's tone sharpened as his eyebrows came together in the beginning of a frown. "We need to wean them away from their own ignorance, lad, that is really the White Man's burden we carry, you know."

Richard kept the smile on his face, trying hard not to let his expression mirror his wayward thoughts.

In his very, very personal opinion, the greater efficiency of the British Empire only meant more revenues being squeezed out of the Indians while better law and order meant ruthless suppression of any opposition to the Company Sahib or any of their representatives, down to the last man, woman and child.

Unfortunately, Richard had committed the cardinal error of voicing his then nascent doubts about the benefits of British oversight for the Indians very early on in his India posting and had at that time faced an immediate and harsh tongue lashing from the erstwhile British resident in front of his peers, which was followed up with a private threat of being returned home in disgrace if he continued to espouse any further thoughts that his superior officers deemed as treason against Her Majesty's government.

He had also coincidentally faced a mysterious blanking out of his social life at around that same time. Suddenly, there were no invitations to any of the almost daily soirees and dances which kept the European community engaged in Lucknow, which not only left the very young man desolate and bereft of company but also led his household servants to view him with thinly disguised pity. This social draught had lasted for a month, after which Richard had slowly ingratiated himself back into the heart of the community. But it had been a lonely period and he was not about to rake all that up again.

He had instead tried to quietly go about the task of restoring a little bit of balance through small acts of support and kindness. This involved promoting the old Bengali babu to another meaningless designation in the resident's office to augment his meagre salary, sending the bright Parsee legal intern to Bombay for additional training, setting aside a bit of funds from the bloated payroll for the Hindoo marriages of the children of the many residency employees, and adjusting farm taxes as much as he could in the last year's poor monsoon. All this made him much beloved of the natives, but it was an uphill struggle every day.

"So, how do you want me to approach the Swami today, sir?" Richard asked, to try and change the topic and bring the conversation safely back to work.

Sir Henry nodded briskly at the reminder and sat up, calling out loudly for his aide-de-camp, Henry Sutcliffe. The overburdened and shy Mr Sutcliffe must have been waiting anxiously around the corner for his cue, for he appeared rapidly with an armload of papers wrapped in red muslin to denote an East India Company file; and the next hour was spent in a detailed discussion, with Richard taking copious notes in his neat copperplate handwriting.

Richard was still mulling over these discussions an hour later as the residency phaeton rattled over the cobbled streets of Lucknow towards his home.

Ever since that fateful day three decades ago when Lord Macaulay had convinced the House of Lords back home in England to root out the local systems of education and impose basic English education as an aspiration for the natives, there had been sweeping changes forcefully made to the educational landscape across the parts of India controlled by the East India

Company. Wresting land and property away from Indian Gurukuls, taxing them at exorbitant rates, arresting well-known gurus, allowing Company jobs to only those schooled in rudimentary English in Company-sanctioned schools—a whole host of measures had been implemented by successive governors to try and undermine the educational framework that had stood Indians in good stead for quite a long while.

The Company believed (as supported by Her Majesty's government) that once the basis of ancient Indian education could be shaken, once they could be forced to believe that they could progress and enrich themselves only through Western (English) literacy, that Indians could be better subjugated and put to work to serve the Company.

And yet, despite tireless efforts on the part of Company officials, the deep roots of the Gurukul system steadfastly refused to be completely wiped out. Significant parts of the wealthy and powerful elements of Indian society still sent their children to Gurukul-type educational institutions all over the north, east and west of India, clinging to their traditional values and mores, focused on peaceful coexistence, which in itself posed a cultural and philosophical counterpoint to the Company's approach of divide and rule through promotion of narrow self-interest.

So now, there was a Company-wide initiative to accelerate the change. Ruthlessly.

And it had been made Richard's responsibility to use all means at his disposal to undermine and arrogate the largest remaining such institution in Lucknow, the Vidyapeeth run by Swami Kiritanand on the banks of the Gomti just outside the city. This institution was a decided thorn in the side of the Company administration since the Vidyapeeth had a centuries-old reputation and it had educated most of the leaders of Indian society in and around Lucknow, and continued to be a strong influence on the thinking of the times with an unfortunate nationalistic bent of mind.

While Richard was coming to the uneasy realisation that a moral dilemma had been thrust upon him, in Sir Henry's mind, the situation was on the contrary further simplified by the fact that the chairman of the Board of Trustees for La Martiniere College (and Sir Henry's hunting partner and close friend) Sir Arthur Rowe highly valued the Vidyapeeth land and wanted to annex it to the already sprawling La Martiniere estate. This congruence of goals, notwithstanding the impact, made it a doubly righteous cause for the British resident.

Richard slowly put away his notes into the rich handcrafted leather valise that his wife had gotten him as a New Year's gift as the carriage swept into the driveway of the sprawling white stucco mansion that he had been allotted. A couple of liveried stable hands came running as the carriage halted under the porch, while Richard's butler and the head of the household servants, Abdul Qadir, hurried down the steps as much as his rotund proportions and sense of self-importance would allow.

"Why is that fellow here? Isn't he an outhouse servant?" Richard asked irritably as Abdul Qadir gently helped his clubfoot land on the ground.

He was referring to Kurnoo, a relatively new addition to the household, who had quietly followed Abdul Qadir's imposing girth down the stairs of the house. Generally an even-tempered man, Richard was not sure what it was about this particular servant that annoyed him—whether it was the light skin and green eyes that set him apart from all the other servants with their warm brown skins and dark eyes; or the fact that he was the only one other than Abdul Qadir who did not always keep his head obsequiously bowed in the presence of his English master; or maybe it was that he constantly gave off the faint aroma of fresh lemons, while Richard was always concerned that he himself smelt of perspiration on hot days despite all the lotions and powders his wife plied him with.

Abdul Qadir bowed obsequiously and replied in a placatory tone, "Sahib, he was watering the *chiks* in memsahib's windows as she wanted to cool the room to sleep. Kurnoo is skilled at this since his father was a chik maker. And you know, Sahib, our two most experienced footmen have now been transferred to serve the British Residency, so he was the best person for the job."

Richard grinned despite himself. He could make out from Abdul Qadir's tone and stiff back that the faithful fellow was still offended at his staff being conscripted to serve another British officer, no matter how much senior than Richard the said officer might be. Richard thought about explaining again to Abdul Qadir, but then shrugged off the matter rather than get into a debate with the fellow; Abdul Qadir was a highly competent butler but suffered from a decidedly exaggerated notion of his own and his master's importance to the British Empire, which in Richard's mind did not need any encouragement at all; and so he went into the house with his awkward rolling gait, heading for his dressing room.

On the way, he peeped into his wife's bedroom, which was cool and dark with the freshly moistened chiks pulled down across the windows. He stopped for a moment and leaned his hip gently against the door jamb, listening to her steady, rhythmic breathing and smiled. To him it sounded as flawless as she looked, with her dimpled face and lithe young feminine body.

Despite the fact that they had been married for over two years and had a year-old son together, he still felt a rush of blood that the luminously beautiful Miss Katherine Scott, daughter of the most powerful merchant family in Lucknow, was now Mrs Richard Lytton-Whyte.

In fact, when he first set his eyes on her at the British resident's garden soiree, Richard had been amazed at his own good fortune that she was still sitting unasked while all the other girls were primly dancing with eligible young bachelors. He had taken a strong gulp of brandy and then had taken all his courage in his hands when he limped up to her and asked her to dance; and was not only richly rewarded with her gracious acceptance but even more important to him, no matter how clumsily he performed on the dance floor, she never glanced at or spoke about his clubfoot the entire evening. Or indeed any of the many evenings they spent speaking together in the many social gatherings that sparkled in Lucknow for the European community.

He was then too new and bereft of feminine family or connections to know the speculation swirling around Lucknow Society about her alleged bold escapades—he was simply and immediately swept away by her incandescent beauty. And her powerful, socially aspirational, merchant-born parents were duly grateful that a bachelor of high birth could see nothing else.

It was true that the then British resident had pursed his lips and contemplated him for a long moment with furrowed brows, when Richard asked his permission to marry Miss Katherine Scott. But the wily old politician had been growing his career in the colonies for a while and he carefully weighed the benefits of being honest with his new, fresh-faced officer against the decided advantage of having the Scott family wealth on his side during the upcoming political skirmishes with the Lucknow Nawabs.

As was normally the case, narrow self-interest won out and the British resident acquiesced to the nuptials of the Right Honourable Richard Lytton-Whyte with Miss Katherine Scott.

For all practical purposes, Richard's parents had no choice in the matter, as the overjoyed and very keen Mr Scott arranged a whirlwind wedding. While the twelfth Earl of Wincombe and his lady received the letter from Richard less than a week before his wedding date and were thus unable to join in the nuptials, they were consoled to know of the Scott family fortune, since Richard as the third son and fifth child of an Earl would gain nothing much other than goodwill and powerful brothers as an inheritance.

Coming back to the present with a small start, Richard gently shut the door to Katherine's room so as not to disturb her sleep. As he limped towards his room, he commanded Abdul Qadir to prepare his travel carriage, instructing him to also bring a change of boots and his formal wig for the journey to the Vidyapeeth.

"And pack some luncheon as well, it will be late before I return," he called out, knowing that a sumptuous spread would be carefully prepared in a huge basket of which he would at best pick a half-dozen bites.

He turned for a moment as he heard the raucous cry of the peacocks in their extensive garden. Looking out on the rolling lush green landscaped acres around him, he remembered his promise to take a peacock and peahen back home to England next winter on his furlough—the first time since his marriage and the birth of their son.

Home was the mid-sized but extremely wealthy estate of Wincombe, a few hours' ride southwest of London, where Richard was the fifth child of the twelfth Earl of Wincombe to be born in the rambling country house, a house in which it was said the grim great hall and its immediate surrounding rooms were built at the time of William the Conqueror, with rambling additions made by subsequent generations whenever the financial resources were available and the current lord of the manor felt the urge to leave his imprint on the family seat.

Richard's four elder siblings had been born to the gentleman farmer Albert Lytton-Whyte, a distant cousin to the eleventh Earl of Wincombe. And to his lady wife, Mistress Fiona, a strong-minded individual with her feet planted as firmly on the ground as a penurious pastor's daughter needed to have. Once she had set her heart on the giant, shy Albert during Sunday school lessons in their late teen years, it took but a short and awkward courtship before the young Albert Lytton-Whyte found himself a married and contented man.

It took almost a decade of marriage, four children, an intervening war, a curricle-racing accident and an alcoholic death disposing of the three intervening heirs before the title of the twelfth Earl of Wincombe was suddenly bestowed on Albert. With his bluff manner, rich knowledge of farming and deep integrity, he set to work to repair the ravages on the estate caused by his profligate predecessors. And by the time Richard was born, almost another decade later, Wincombe was one of the wealthiest estates in the country, earning the twelfth Earl a strong voice in the House of Lords.

When the by now heavy-set Albert walked gently in to see the accidental new-born Richard, he found Lady Fiona cradling the child with a furrowed brow. As he gently stroked the auburn curls back from her forehead, she raised her tear-soaked eyes to him and lifted the swaddling cloth away from the baby so his deformed clubfoot was visible.

"We should not have had him so late in our lives, our eldest daughter is already betrothed to be married. This is our punishment..." Lady Fiona said in a choked voice.

Albert stared in dismay at the child, thinking of the many activities that he could never join in and the lifetime of shame and name-calling that he would have to endure. He stood there wordless for a long moment and then he patted the baby's stomach in an absent-minded way. As his simple heart filled with helpless despair, he started to turn away...

...and stopped.

His hand was stuck.

As he turned back, he saw that his little son had grasped his forefinger with a strong unyielding grip, a grip that no new-born should have. Even as he tugged several times, he was unable to break the bondage of those little hands.

A slow smile broke through the concern that clouded his face as Albert turned back to Fiona and said in a choked voice, "He'll do, lass. He'll do."

And Richard did.

Raised with bottomless affection from his elder siblings and his father and with absolute protective adoration by his mother, Richard was surrounded by people who never let him feel his physical affliction during his formative years. He knew he was less fleet of foot than average, of course, but he was raised to also know that he had an agility of mind and a strength of heart that would stand him in better stead.

While growing up in the midst of great wealth, he was nevertheless imbued with all the good, honest values that a gentleman farmer and a pastor's daughter could impart.

And he rewarded them all as only he could.

Richard participated in every activity he could and many he could not. He was smaller than his giant elder brothers and strapping father, but his energy was boundless. He swam, hunted, fished, rode and farmed with them all, as they tutored him together, although he was never great in any of these activities. Fencing, dancing, foot races were all beyond him, but he remained undaunted even as he accepted his failures.

Richard was exceptional with animals on the farm, especially with the estate dogs and horses, with many hours happily spent in the stables during his childhood.

But his outstanding qualities were empathy and tenacity, all bound in relentless good cheer.

When Ostler Wilkins's son was lost in the woods, Richard stayed with the search party till dawn when they found the child on the verge of exhausted collapse. When the farmers faced years of bad crops, he pleaded their case energetically with his lord father and brothers, always coming back with small victories to help the poor. And he poured his heart and soul into his studies with the family tutor and became the first member of his branch of the family to join and graduate from Harrow.

After two years chasing a degree in Oxford, his lord father mooted the idea of buying an executive post in the East India Company for Richard, much to the discomfiture of Lady Fiona and her two daughters. But Richard realised that his father was opening up a rare chance to make his fortune. In his optimism, he foresaw a glittering career as an administrator, which was at that time second only to a gentleman officer's command in the army. Since the army would never have him with his congenital deformity, the Company was an alternative gateway to the magical land of India, where he could make his name and fortune—something much more difficult to do in England as the third son of an Earl.

And so it was that on an overcast summer's day in 1854, Richard waved from the deck of his ship to his family and his receding homeland as the vessel pulled away slowly for the long voyage to Calcutta, from where he would travel over land on horseback and carriage to his Company posting in Lucknow. Although he did not know it yet, he would not return for the next three years, caught up as he would be in work, a whirlwind romance and marriage and the subsequent birth of his own son and heir…

As the carriage rumbled back in the early evening on its way back from the Vidyapeeth, Richard stared despondently out of the curtained window at the darkening lush greenery on both sides, slumped back in the plump, wine-coloured leather seat.

The meeting had ended prematurely, with the Vidyapeeth authorities courteous but firm, offering almost no chance of any compromise. He admired the unique work being done there to educate young Indian children and imbue them with ancient values, but he knew that if they did not agree to relocate to a much smaller property and start offering British education classes, the Company would unleash a range of legal and administrative tactics which would render them helpless and challenge their very existence.

Since he was returning a good couple of hours earlier than planned, Richard leant forward and told his coachman Ajju to take the carriage in through the side entrance and go directly to the stables. Ajju was used to these requests; he knew that his sahib loved his horses and enjoyed brushing them down in the stables because it gave him a sense of his own childhood spent blissfully amongst estate animals. It was one of the things that made his sahib more human than the other *Angrez*, one of the many ways in which he was like them, one of the many ways his kindness shone through—which was why they all trusted and cared for him.

The sun had already set. Despite the darkness, the lanterns at the side gate were unlit because no visitors were expected this evening who would drive directly to the stables, but Ajju and his horses knew the way well enough, so they picked their way through to the stables quietly in the dim glow of the carriage lantern.

Various constellations of stars had begun their conquest of the moonless sky by the time Richard—his spirits lifted by an hour of honest exertion unbridling and brushing down the tired horses—slung his greatcoat and tails over his shoulder and strolled in his shirtsleeves to the narrow winding internal spiral staircase which led from the stables to the main mansion. It was even darker than the surrounding moonless garden and brutally steep since it was only meant for the Indian servants, but Richard preferred it to the long walk around to the front of the house.

Unfortunately, halfway up the steps, the darkness defeated him.

As Richard's awkward clubfoot missed a high and uneven step in the dark, he suddenly tripped and fell heavily on his hands, momentarily knocking the air out of his lungs. He stopped himself from tumbling further by grabbing hard the steps with his hands, but he could feel the warm wetness of blood oozing out through multiple lacerations on his palms and his head was swimming from being slammed against the wall.

As he tried to shake off the shock and pushed on his trembling arms to stand up, his breath caught again in his throat.

He heard a stealthy tread on the stairs below him, coming ever closer. Not the confident springing steps of a servant going to serve his masters, but a shuffling creeping whisper of sound, made by someone trying not be discovered.

He sat quickly on a step, still trembling all over, and looked down. In the velvety blackness enveloping the staircase, he could barely make out a very dim silhouette in pale clothes coming around the spiralling darkness a little below him.

All the stories he had heard of vicious thugs stalking and killing wealthy Europeans in their sleep came rushing back into his mind. The side gate had been dark and unguarded, who knew what dreadful felon had crept in after him?

"Who's that?" He called out in a low rasping unrecognisable harsh whisper from his suddenly dry throat.

The pale silhouette stopped moving with a shocking suddenness, but whether to attack or flee, Richard did not wait to find out. He lashed out with his foot, landing a blow with all his weight behind it. There was a high-pitched piercing scream, a loud sickening crack of bone suddenly meeting stone and the dim silhouette tumbled around a bend in the staircase.

There was a long moment of silence, as if everything in the world had stopped to see what would happen next.

Then a hubbub of many sounds broke out in the servants' quarters next door.

Richard raised himself shakily on his aching knee and stood, drawing shuddering breaths, swaying on his feet, a fleeting citrus scent drifting past his nose. Then, holding the wall, he stumbled his way back down the curving stairs.

Made even more grotesque by the ebb and flow of light from the many bobbing lanterns held aloft by the gathering servants at the bottom of the stairs, a horrific sight met his eyes. Katherine lay sprawled on her back across the uneven floor in her pink satin nightclothes, her shapely body badly bent in an unnatural position, her lustrous hair streaming across the stones, getting wetter by the moment with the viscous blood flowing slowly from her broken skull.

A low, involuntary moan escaped Richard as he collapsed on his haunches in front of his wife's corpse. He moaned again and shook his head, then he looked up slowly from her sightless eyes…

… to look directly into Kurnoo's rage-filled, maddened ones.

Then Kurnoo leapt at him, swinging his lantern in a long looping arc, as Abdul Qadir vainly reached out to clutch at the younger man.

Richard's last odd thought was *The old devil was right, the revolution is here…*

And then his world turned black.

The next morning, on a misty morning in a faraway Barrackpore parade ground, sepoy Mangal Pandey of the 34th BNI attacked his British officers and signalled the beginning of the First Indian War of Independence.

6

Source Code

Despite the soundless chill of the powerful air conditioning, Ravi Kapoor was perspiring lightly with adrenaline-charged energy as he strode back to his managing director's office from the bank's impressive boardroom.

The Board Audit and Risk Subcommittee had not commenced on an auspicious note. There were the usual noises about KYC for standalone cardholders and money laundering thresholds of corporate remittances and whole ream of monitoring statistics with the usual set of lacunae. The Treasury Operations team had unexpectedly introduced an emerging concern, where they had observed an unforeseen spike in their outward USD remittances, leading to a rare breach of the limits imposed on their overnight position by the Risk Management team.

But eventually, after discussing all the other agenda items, the Subcommittee came to the review report covering the long planned, transformational and massive transaction banking systems conversion which had been completed the previous month. All the User Acceptance Testing checkpoints had been passed with practically no adverse customer impact, a few reported glitches had been resolved before the rollout to the entire bank.

This vaunted new system was intended to take the bank into the next few decades of growth with optimum digital processing—a huge step forward for the bank as well as tremendous content for its advertising campaigns in traditional and social media. The Board Audit Committee went through the report diligently, with every member of the Committee lavish in their personal praise for the success of this lengthy, ambitious project. Of course, Ravi, as the Chief Operating Officer of the International Commercial & Investment Bank (or ICI Bank) and the management sponsor of the entire project, had naturally basked in glory for the remainder of the meeting.

Quite apart from the bank's implementation team, it had been the external vendor's strong execution focus and technical support which had enabled this success—even bringing the entire project within the deadline and below the originally estimated budget. And everyone knew that Janus Technologies had been hand-picked by Ravi after a year-long, arduous selection process.

The COO cut an impressive figure as he walked briskly down the thickly carpeted corridor, a big powerfully built man in an impeccable Savile Row charcoal pinstripe suit, the dull maroon Hermes tie matching his kerchief, an expensive haircut cleverly disguising the thinning top. As he reached the imposing wood-panelled doors of his room, his secretary Brenda bustled out from behind her neat desk to waylay him.

"Ravi, I am so sorry, but I have to speak to you before your next meeting. There is a furious client at Reception, he is a Wealth Management customer, an elderly gentleman, and he is absolutely demanding to see you. It seems he has had an excess charge of 50 rupees on his personal account and he is saying it has never happened before in all his life."

Seeing his darkening expression, she hastily continued, "I know, I know; the branch should have handled it downstairs, but they sent him up because he is the MD of Cartwright Engineering, one of our big corporate clients."

Ravi stopped in front of his office door, mentally calculating whether this could be useful for him.

Deciding against it, he waved dismissively at Brenda. "Call Subir from his office, he is the regional head for West, make sure he resolves it—get him to confirm by this evening," he said brusquely. "Oh, and please apologise to the client for me, use all your pretty words."

As she turned to go, Ravi remembered something else. "Wait… wait, Brenda…Take a business card from my desk to give him." He winked at her playfully. "Go ahead, get going, I like to see you walk in front of me…"

Brenda smiled dutifully, but the stiffness of her back revealed her discomfort as she entered his plush office with giant bay windows overlooking the sparkling blue waters of the Arabian Sea. Three of his department heads were already seated on the sofa, waiting for Ravi so that they could commence their monthly review of the bank's overseas subsidiaries.

Brenda collected the business card, asked about coffee and then left the office to do as she had been bidden by her boss, who was a stickler for obedience and would expect a full report after his review.

As the presentation began on a state-of-the-art, curved, 60-inch high-definition screen, Ravi settled back into the luxurious leather sofa, his agile mind already switching gears, preparing to ask the uncomfortable questions and ruthlessly impose discipline to ensure things got done.

In a few hours, Malini and he would board a flight to Dubai. It would be his first real break in over a year and he was greatly looking forward to it—the reunion of old, familiar batchmates at Sanjay's place, the rounds of night golf, the profusion of single malt and cigars, meeting new people and (very important to Ravi) showcasing his own success.

But first, he had a review to complete and he focused all his intense energy on it.

So many of them had met each other on the same occasion, that fateful early summer's day a little more than two decades ago.

Ravi, Malini, Sanjay, of course.

And Subbu.

A nervous group of freshly recruited young MBAs and CAs had gathered on the twenty-eighth floor of Bakhtawar Tower in Nariman Point in Mumbai, in the posh conference room of the First American Bank, the biggest and most powerful foreign bank in India.

A few young men from hardcore engineering backgrounds, wearing sober suits and holding files or bags of their personal documents, clustered together near the foot of the table. As a group, they looked vaguely uncomfortable in their new environment, their conversation drying up after the initial muttered introductions.

A handful of young women sat separately and demurely in front, apparently trying not to convey any first impressions which they could regret later. The remaining few girls, led by the vivacious Malini Bhattacharya, were busy getting acquainted with the rest of the room, introducing themselves and shaking hands formally.

Ravi breezed in just before nine, immediately clasping hands warmly and patting shoulders, working the room like a seasoned people manager, befitting a married man with prior work experience. His course around the room brought him to a stop in front of a fresh-faced, bespectacled fellow wearing a slightly mismatched navy blue jacket and trousers, who was gazing vacantly out of the window towards the horizon.

"Hi there, buddy, I'm Ravi, how're you doing?" Ravi repeated cheerfully, holding out his right hand.

The young man with the spectacles continued looking out of the window as if he had not heard, causing Ravi to hesitate. He spoke again, questioningly, "Hi there, all OK…?"

Just as Ravi shrugged and turned away, he heard a soft, slow, nasal drawl behind him. "I guess you are Ravi Kapoor, top three in your batch in IIM Bangalore, right? You were offered treasury but picked consumer banking—probably on good advice, because I read that your dad is a banker. Come on, man," the voice continued in a reproachful tone, "you're being just too chirpy for the first day."

That was Ravi's introduction to Sanjay Gokhale, the eldest son of the Gokhale family which owned the giant conglomerate, G Tech Industries. A brilliant albeit eccentric young man, more than making up in intellectual pedigree what he lacked in social skills. Now a trainee at the First Bank of America to learn the financing aspect of the business as a result of a gentleman's agreement between the G Tech Industries board and the bank's management.

Ravi turned back with a surprised, spontaneous grin, to begin a lifelong friendship.

The hum of desultory conversation around the room quietened suddenly as Sujit Talwar, the India CEO of the First Bank of America entered, followed by the heads of HR, Corporate Banking, Treasury and Consumer Banking.

The newbies who had been standing suddenly scuttled around, trying to find a seat near a friendly face. Ravi, typically, made a beeline for the prettiest girl in the room, sitting between Malini Bhattacharya and a pale, shy-looking girl who would in future years go on to set up the first Sovereign Risk Modelling department in the bank.

The usual medley of encouragingly worded welcome speeches and packaged career advice followed for the next ninety minutes, along with the mandatory PowerPoint slides. As the Head of HR brought the formal presentations to a close and asked everyone to pick up coffee and sandwiches from the neatly laid out counters at the side before the Q&A session, she added ceremoniously, "We are so proud to welcome all of you from India's premier MBA institutes and fresh chartered accountants…" She stopped and looked down the table towards the group seated at the other end. "A warm welcome also to the topper from Kellogg School who joins us this year—Subbu, great to have you, won't you stand up to let everyone know who you are?"

Venkatakrishnan Subramanian, a pale, tall and gauntly good-looking young man with intense eyes behind rimless spectacles, stood up reluctantly, clearly uncomfortable at being singled out, and sat down again quickly, as a little murmur went around the room.

As they settled back with their coffee and sandwiches, Sujit Talwar looked around with a professional smile and asked, "Any more questions?"

There was a moment's awkward silence as everyone looked around, waiting for someone else to take the plunge; then, Ravi's hand shot up.

"Sir, Ravi Kapoor from IIM Bangalore. Sir, we have been lucky over the past few years, but in your opinion, how long will the current growth rate sustain? And how can we, as a bank and as incoming staff, leverage it?" He asked confidently.

"No marks for class participation here," someone in the room said in a hoarse stage whisper, causing a little ripple of nervous laughter.

Sujit Talwar smiled cursorily at the whisper and then nodded approvingly in Ravi's direction to set the tone. "Good question, Ravi…" he said, proceeding to answer in detail, talking about demand-led growth, FDI flows, currency and interest rates and the bank's strategic positioning, bringing in the business heads to speak on specific points from time to time.

All the management trainees listened, with varying degrees of attentiveness. It was clear to all of them that the CEO was on home ground and feeling good about sharing his grand vision with the gathered group of neophytes; everyone also registered that the big man now knew who Ravi was!

Ravi, of course, had been prepared well in advance, because he knew that that there are always marks for class participation, especially where senior professional egos were involved. And far from being concerned about the jealousy and annoyance it sometimes earned him from his peers, he relished the opportunity to stand out.

This brash, politically savvy style was to become his hallmark as Ravi determinedly climbed the rungs of the corporate ladder over the next couple of decades.

The 1994 batch of management trainees was one of the most tightly knit batches the bank had ever seen, even though it was the largest intake of trainees in its history as the bank was committing itself to accelerated growth in India.

A new bank-wide email and internal messaging platform was implemented that year, which meant the whole batch stayed in touch constantly, sometimes right in the middle of meetings—enjoying a joke, helping each other with data, staying connected with office gossip. And the core of the batch remained in Mumbai, partying together on most nights, covering for each other's hangover absences in the office, forming an immediate support group when anyone suffered a bereavement, sharing chummeries, splitting bills and competing wholeheartedly for promotions which the bank distributed feely at the junior levels as a means of retention and motivation.

Sanjay Gokhale was from the very beginning clearly the oddball of the batch, with his mismatched clothes, extremely finicky food habits, unfiltered and disturbingly honest personal comments about others (always directly, never behind their back), daydreaming during meetings (yet recalling every word spoken), reading quantum physics for relaxation instead of partying… Yet he was peerless in what he did, consuming vast amounts of data quickly, deciphering patterns and identifying trends that others couldn't even see, joining treasury and quickly becoming a currency-trading powerhouse before setting up the bank's private equity fund.

Malini remained the heartbeat of the batch, her strong people proclivities leading her to a talent management role in HR. She always took care to connect the reclusive Sanjay to the others, but rarely saw eye to eye with Ravi, loudly complaining in a good-natured way to his face about his consistent aggression. She was courted by many senior managers (some married, others not) because of her classical good looks, her positive energy and her popularity, but she herself had a soft corner for the gentle, reclusive Subbu, who had been conscripted by the management into a visionary project to establish a pioneering Internet-based desktop banking program.

While this affection on her part made everyone smile, the shy and work-focused Subbu found Malini's attention uncomfortable, though flattering. But his equilibrium was disturbed when his mother passed away at a very young age—less than a couple of years after his joining the bank. Since he had lost his father at an early age, he was devastated for months because he had returned to India only for his mother's sake. During these dark days, Malini's strong and supportive presence helped him rediscover his emotional moorings. Their companionship blossomed with a slow intensity and the two were quietly married the following year.

A few batchmates went overseas on 'money' assignments, to Singapore, Hongkong and more recently to Dubai, which was a fast-growing centre. Subbu continued his digital journey, building a software subsidiary for the bank which would service their global operations. Malini grew apace within the HR domain, while Sanjay made millions for the bank and himself first in currencies and later in a proprietary equity fund. But Ravi took every growth opportunity, even undertaking a business audit in Fiji for six weeks in extremely testing circumstances, while he built his CV for his big break.

Throughout their initial years of growth, the batch of 1994 continued to remain an amazingly tight-knit group.

Until the team building offsite of 2002.

It was an extended three-day affair at a luxurious Goa resort. With a new young American CEO at the helm, everyone realised they were being figured out for senior roles. This added a sharp edge to the gruelling team-building activities, which carried on late into the first night. Presentations from 8 o'clock the next morning tested both stamina and aspiration of all the teams; so by the time the Gala Awards night arrived, most people were close to being emotionally and physically drained.

Spouses were invited for the awards night; many had flown in specifically for it while a few had been chilling in the resort from the beginning. As one of the organisers, when Sanjay ambled into the refreshment centre early with his plump, cheerful wife Vaidehi to go over the arrangements one last time with the event manager, he was startled to find Ravi's wife Maya already there, a lone figure sitting at one of the many beautifully laid out dinner tables, intoxicated and slurring angrily.

She completely ignored their affectionate greetings and immediately asked about 'that bloody Malini'.

"What the hell is going on between my husband and that bitch?" Maya burst out before they could reply, as if she had been brooding about it and could not bring her mind to focus on anything else. "His bloody phone is full of her texts and pictures, and he just goddamn disappears whenever she calls—this is so much bloody bullshit!"

Sanjay's relaxed tiredness quickly dissipated as he realised they were dealing with someone on the verge of losing control. "Relax Maya, just take a deep breath, my dear," he said reassuringly as Vaidehi moved to put her arm around Maya's shoulders. "Do you really believe there could be anything going on between the two of them. Maybe a little bit of healthy flirting, don't you think?"

"Flirting? Healthy flirting? What the bloody hell, Sanjay!" Maya rolled her eyes in disgust. "That's what you men call it? There is nothing healthy about running to the guest bedroom to take long calls in the middle of the night, or missing family occasions to spend time with a female colleague or rearranging your schedule constantly to take office trips together!"

Maya shook off Vaidehi's arm impatiently and got up from her seat to walk unsteadily around the table, gesticulating and muttering in a low, angry voice to herself. Suddenly, she stopped, turned back, looked at Sanjay and asked bluntly, "Sanjay—please be absolutely honest with me, did my husband sleep with her? You are his friend. Did he ever tell you anything about it?"

With her pleading eyes holding his own, Sanjay's unfortunate streak of candour surfaced suddenly. "Come on, Maya. You need to relax please, the whole bank will be here soon. Even if Malini and Ravi are sleeping together, freaking out now won't help…" he said gently, trying in his own way to defuse the situation, just as Subbu and Malini strolled into the room.

Subbu stopped dead, his gaunt face with its now receding hairline suddenly draining of all colour. He turned slowly towards Malini, his hands clenched tightly, trembling visibly. Malini stared back at him wide-eyed for an aching, interminable moment, her eyes brimming, caught unawares, speechless, the answer to his unspoken question written large in her stricken expression.

Then Subbu stumbled away without a backward glance.

That was the moment the batch of 1994 started to fall apart.

❧

Sanjay and Vaidehi now lived in a palatial mansion in the posh Emirates Hills in Dubai, as befit the CEO and managing director of the global overseas operations of G Tech Industries.

Malini walked out with Vaidehi through the back door and across the parquet-floored veranda into the chilly night air, where the huge garden was transformed with hidden lighting in the flower bushes and the flickering flames of *mashaals* around the edges; the mouth-watering aroma of grilled meats and vegetables wafted from the barbecue that Sanjay had organised for the reunion dinner in honour of Ravi and Malini.

There had been a few moments of awkwardness earlier when one of their old friends had raised a toast to Subbu, who had passed away in the US a few weeks back. Almost all of them had turned instinctively towards Malini, but she had graciously raised her glass as well, the expression on her beautiful face clouding with genuine sorrow. A conversation had started about Subbu's huge success with funding tech start-ups in the recent past, but Ravi had in his usual blustering style changed the topic and any nostalgic remembrances of Subbu were swept aside.

The men were now all clustered around the canopied poolside bar, happily drunk, singing bawdy songs like they all used to in their twenties.

Vaidehi squeezed Malini's arm affectionately. "He looks quite relaxed now, Malini, you really kept him busy with friends and shopping… oh, and the amusement park with the kids the whole day, good on you, girl."

"Thanks sweetie, you and Sanjay are such terrific hosts," Malini responded warmly. "He had been so badly stressed out over the past few months, we really needed this break—and all your company."

"Not to forget the contribution of all that single malt to the mellow moods of our immature men…" chuckled Vaidehi.

Malini turned to her with a mischievous smile. "And most important, I got Ravi to switch off his office phone with the email and give it to me for the weekend, so that nothing distracts him!"

Others joined them and the conversation moved on to their many shared memories and the turns their lives had taken after they had last seen each other.

The evening stretched cheerfully and loudly into the late night and then into the early hours of the next morning before the last guests dragged themselves off, reluctant to leave such a wonderful evening, replete with great music, fabulous food and drink and the nostalgic company of old friends. Ravi needed all Malini's help to stumble up the stairs to the bedrooms, with Sanjay climbing behind in case Ravi fell back, while Vaidehi supervised the clean-up by the tired servants downstairs. It was almost dawn before the whole household was sound asleep.

The sun was past the noon mark in the sky the next morning when Ravi walked out onto the rear veranda, where Sanjay was at work on his laptop over a post-breakfast cup of coffee. Sanjay looked up at his old friend, who was clean-shaven and bright-eyed, none the worse for wear for the previous night's activities. "Well, well—good morning, you are looking bright and chirpy today..." he greeted Ravi.

Ravi grinned, sitting down and switching on the iPhone in his hand. "Great party last night, buddy. Plus I grabbed my work phone from Malini's purse while she is still asleep. I can quickly catch up on what's happening before she wakes up."

Sanjay got up to pour Ravi some coffee from the decanter on the trolley at the side. "Do you still take it with milk...?" He turned to ask, but was interrupted by a loud yelp of surprise from Ravi, who was staring at his mobile with a horrified expression as it pinged furiously with accumulated text messages and emails arriving in a heap.

The full extent of the damage unfolded only after about half an hour, after Ravi had skimmed though the most important messages. By that time, Vaidehi had returned from the gym and Malini had joined them all on the veranda, standing behind Ravi with a stricken expression, her hand on his shoulder.

The new operating system implemented by ICI Bank had gone rogue. It had been debiting every one of the bank's over twelve million customers with amounts ranging from fifty to a thousand rupees, accumulating the amounts in dummy accounts and then remitting overseas in US dollars through the automated remittance module. Ravi's face turned ashen as he realised he should have looked more closely at the customer complaint before leaving and that they should have all paid more attention to the treasury concerns about USD remittances in the Board Audit Committee.

The bank had apparently tried all they could, but the vendor's subcontracted IT developers who had customised the product was uncontactable.

As was the managing director and COO of ICI Bank, whose phone had been switched off.

"Why didn't they go back to the source code? Trace the malware?" Vaidehi asked, a former banker herself.

Ravi looked up wearily. "That is the core of my problem, Vaidehi. I squeezed a great deal out of Janus Technologies, in return for which I allowed them to keep the source code for a month after implementation—so that they could hardcode the learnings from our customisation and use it for other clients outside India... By the time we get the source code, it will be wiped clean so that they never have any culpability..."

He buried his head in his hands with a groan. "Oh God...I am finished... finished!"

Sanjay looked up grimly from the laptop, where he had busied himself over the past half-hour as the drama unfolded. "Dear God... He was always so clever..." he said, almost to himself.

Ravi was totally absorbed in his despair, but both the women turned to Sanjay.

"What is it?" Malini asked, with a foreboding of dread.

Sanjay sighed. "It is not easy to find, but if you look for it hard enough..." His voice tapered off as he met Malini's eyes. "Janus Technologies was Subbu's last start-up investment before he died," he said, the sadness in his voice unmistakable.

7

To Cut a Long Story Short

On an overcast wintry morning in the posh, upmarket colony of Shanti Niketan in Delhi, as the sun feebly tried to impose itself on the reluctantly wakening city, the Azizi household was already abuzz with activity.

Their eldest daughter was getting married.

At last.

Salma was an imperious beauty, an established clinical psychiatrist, the first-born of the four Azizi siblings and very much the apple of her father's eye. Her steadfast refusal to get married even while her younger siblings all settled down had been extremely vexatious for Mrs Azizi, and in the last couple of years, even had the doting Mr Azizi deeply concerned. But all that was behind them now as she had capitulated a few months ago; and Mrs Azizi, to her eternal relief, had discovered that there were many eligible Muslim South Asian men still looking for a bride in her thirties.

The sprawling mansion was overflowing with family. Family retainers were serving breakfast and ferrying copious amounts of sweet tea to the rooms as the elders finished their *fajr* prayers. The teenagers had been forced to renew their family ties by being bundled together in two adjoining rooms, from where the strains of good-natured disputes over toilets could be heard, along with loud inappropriate music.

Mrs Azizi was on the phone, volubly giving conflicting instructions to her driver, who had been despatched to the airport to pick up her youngest sister's family from Dubai. She had to raise her voice to be heard over the hubbub, which was compounded by the sound of sawing from the neighbour's garden.

Their new neighbours were cutting down the old peepul tree to make way for swings for their three rambunctious toddlers. They had moved in recently after the lady had inherited the house from her distinguished uncle and the previous owner, the rugged Colonel Randhawa, who had tragically died on a peace-keeping mission in Africa. Their lively young family was quite a sharp contrast to the Colonel's very formal, very private persona.

The sound of sawing ceased as a cup of tea made its way out to the gardener. He settled down comfortably on his haunches and gulped down the hot, sweet liquid gratefully, wondering who had tended the tree so carefully that it rose past the garden wall and thrust its strongest branch towards the next door window of the imperiously beautiful lady looking out with sad eyes.

8

Eccentric

The weak, wintry sun was already on its downward journey, accompanied by a few dark, brooding rain clouds drifting aimlessly across the sky. The mellowing sunlight did little to soften the contours of the bleak, inhospitable terrain which spread out as far as the eye could see in an almost unbroken vista of rough-hewn greyish-brown rocks and hillocks, with a few, scattered intermittent clumps of green that clung to precarious life against all odds.

There was almost no movement visible, barring the government jeep jolting and bouncing its way with grim determination along an almost invisible dirt track, leaving a plume of dust in its wake that spiralled and dissipated in the light breeze.

The three men in the jeep clung to their seats with practised unison, bearing the jolting discomfort of their journey in companionable silence. They had already traversed a fair distance during the day together and they had run through their store of family news, gossip and bawdy songs during the long trip.

Constable Sewak Ram at the wheel was the youngest, a large, swarthy, muscular youngster in his almost new uniform, clutching the wheel tightly in his huge hands as he squinted in concentration out of the dust-spattered windscreen, trying his best to avoid the potholes and boulders that the road placed in his path in a continuous stream.

Sewak Ram had barely completed his initiation training a month ago. This was his first real assignment outside the routine drills in the prison grounds, so he was doubly keen to prove he was a worthy addition to the Uttar Pradesh police force.

Head Constable Charan Dass in the backseat was at the other extreme, a grizzled and wrinkled veteran with a greying stubble on his bony chin matching his resplendent white moustache, long, lanky legs spread out in relaxation. He had both Sewak Ram's and his own ancient carbine rifles strapped to his back as he smoked a foul-smelling dark little beedi with his eyes half closed, blowing a thin stream of blue smoke out of the back of the open jeep.

Their commanding officer sat next to Sewak Ram, left leg raised out of the open door, resting on the step, left hand clinging to the frame of the roof under the canvas covering. Inspector Harbans Nat was a trim and dapper little figure in his crisp uniform, his chest adorned with medals for various acts of merit and bravery, his cap in his right hand. His chin rested low on his neck as he gazed at the horizon with a slight smile, imagining and planning all the novel and exciting things he and Sara Ann could do in his imminent next posting.

Charan Dass opened his eyes after a particularly rough bump in the road caused him to slip sideways in his seat and shifted himself into another more comfortable position in his seat. He bent forward slightly to peer out of the windscreen at the setting sun and then smacked Sewak Ram lightly on the back of his head. "You should move a little faster, you giant lump. There is no point reaching after the prisoner has ridden away safely!" He admonished him, half-jokingly.

Inspector Nat raised himself from his reverie and half raised his hand. "No, no, don't worry. No need for that. This is a treacherous road, don't drive any faster than this," he said. "In any case, the only train he can get on to is at 8 p.m., which is two hours away. We will reach in another half-hour, so we have plenty of time," he finished.

"No other train the whole day?" Charan Dass asked in a surprised tone.

"There must be, I guess…" responded Inspector Nat. "But nothing which slows down or stops, so there is no chance of his jumping on to any of them. It is 8 p.m. tonight or nothing."

Young Sewak Ram had been following this exchange with some signs of stress, but at the conclusion, he relaxed slightly and continued rattling along at the same pace.

Charan Dass leaned back and finished the last few puffs of his beedi before throwing it out of the back of the jeep and taking out a large thermos flask. He carefully poured himself half a cup of lukewarm tea and tapped Inspector Nat on the shoulder, who accepted it gratefully and took a couple of sips before handing the cup back. The two men shared the tea for a few minutes in unspoken rapport without any barriers between them, after which Charan

Dass poured a little bit of tea into a small glass bottle and handed it to Sewak Ram.

Nat and Charan Dass shared the same cup without challenging any social protocols as they were from the same caste. Nat had in fact joined as a Constable when Charan Dass was already Head Constable and had been trained and drilled by Charan Dass. But Harbans Nat had been very different from all the other new recruits from the very start.

Inspired by hearing Mahatma Gandhi speak in Lucknow, Harbans's father Chand Ram had been one of the few of his caste who had cast aside the yoke of earning his daily living and joined in the Independence movement against the British. He had marched behind the great man along with hundreds of thousands, accepted beatings from the police, been jailed, had his head and arms broken, suffered debilitating fever but had never lost sight of the land of equality and freedom that Gandhi, Nehru, Patel and the other leaders promised. Chand Ram was one of the many millions who had been filled with hope at the thought of a future that emancipated them from their shackled past and he had imbued his two little children with the same hopes and dreams.

So, from the time that they could speak and understand their father, Harbans and his younger sister Lachhmi had believed that their destiny was not the wretched one of their forefathers, that they were not to be consigned to the bottom of a socio-economic pile simply because of their caste at birth. They believed they could carve out their future with their own hands in the new India that had been born before them.

Harbans had been moved from a government school to a small English-medium private school at an early age, to support which his father worked two jobs in a factory and as a private watchman and his mother swept the houses of the wealthy. Watching his parents' many sacrifices, he pushed himself to overcome all the natural barriers of culture, background, language and acceptance in school to pass out creditably in the middle of the pack. Other boys first attempted to bully him because of his background and limited vernacular language skills, as is the wont of small boys, but found him well able to defend himself with his fists and emotionally almost immune to their taunts.

It cost Harbans a lot of internal trauma to not react harshly, but his father's wise counsel and boundless love every evening made the next day worthwhile. And although he lacked close friends, over the years his steadfast refusal to rise to a bait and his determination to do better than others expected of him earned him the grudging respect of his peers and the unadulterated benevolence of most of his teachers.

Chand Ram's death from a massive heart attack brought on by overwork during the first year of Harbans's college almost broke his spirit. All of a sudden, he felt he had lost his emotional and spiritual anchor and the source of all his strength. He was so absolutely disconsolate that for the first few days after his father's death, he completely lost his moorings, having to be reminded repeatedly by his mother and his sister to bathe, change his clothes and even eat and sleep as he spent his time staring vacantly into the distance with slow tears trickling intermittently down his unshaven face.

He had the shadowy feeling in his heart that Chand Ram would walk in through the door at any time.

Of course, his father didn't.

Yet the feeling of waiting persisted.

Every night, the young Harbans would sit out under the night stars long after the last lamps in his community had gone out, immersed in his grief, hugging his empty world close to his thin chest. Slowly, as the pain of separation numbed with the passing of days, out of the darkness of his grief and the shadowy belief in his still boyish heart was forged a hopeful little conviction, one that gently but firmly took hold of him—a conviction he was still connected to his father's spirit.

This impossible but incandescent belief was a lifeline that Harbans clung to as he slowly regained normality in his everyday life.

He found unexpected support through long and emotional discussions with the neighbourhood temple cleaner, who was a friend of his father's and who passed along all the spiritual wisdom he had gleaned from listening to the priests comforting the wealthy upper-caste patrons who had suffered personal losses.

Bolstered by this belief and the connection to his father that he could feel in his heart, his determination to make his father proud straightened Harbans's back and squared his shoulders afresh.

With his exhausted mother getting more frail and no family savings to fall back upon, Harbans took up the job of a watchman as well, while studying for his college and supporting his younger sister Lachhmi through school. This did nothing for his grades and caused him to fail his IAS entrance exams miserably. Nevertheless, Harbans still became the first person in the family, the village and the caste to graduate from college, thus taking a big step towards fulfilling Chand Ram's dreams for him.

Harbans continued to apply enthusiastically for jobs above his perceived station in life, but after a hapless year of frustrating interviews which inexplicably ended in rejections, he settled for the entry-level police job so many of his family and village friends had taken up before him—even without his college degree.

There were sniggers, of course, jibes from friends and enemies alike—what was the use of the English-medium school, the college degree and Chand Ram's aspirations if the boy was going to do what everyone else did—but Harbans focused on committing absolutely everything to his job, volunteering for the most dangerous assignments, working longer hours without overtime, meeting every senior officer to seek better opportunities while learning and adapting all the time.

Over half a dozen eventful years, Harbans rose quickly in the depleted Lucknow police force, escaping death quite narrowly a few times when they drove into the Chambal in hot pursuit of the notorious dacoits who called it home. But his work was noticed and appreciated by senior officers, so he got promoted as soon as the system would allow, helped immeasurably by his now comfortably spoken English and his college degree.

Lachhmi's determination was unfortunately not as robust as her brother's and her abilities not so developed, so she struggled in school and passed out with marks too low for any reputed college. Wanting to make Chand Ram's dreams for her come true as well, Harbans and Lachhmi explored every possible alternative together. Finally, they were referred to a young trainee nun from Goa who was doing a stint of duty at the local church, a Ms Sara Ann Fernandes, who was using her spare time in a new place by offering to coach school students, and who generously agreed to take on Lachhmi and tutor her for the nurses entrance exam.

Harbans dropped Lachhmi to and picked her up from Sara Ann's church quarters every evening for three months and spent pleasant evenings chatting with his sister's tutor. Mutual respect turned to liking and then evolved quickly into a stronger emotion. Sara Ann found this intense, quiet young man's optimistic vision of the future to be infectious and inspirational, while Harbans was enchanted by Sara Ann's unbending determination and strength which somehow made him feel protective and proud at the same time.

Their meetings became more frequent even after Lachhmi made it into nursing training, causing another social upheaval as they took the immensely courageous decision to get married. While Sara Ann was an orphan and could take her own decisions, the Church apparatus was highly disapproving of Harbans and his family and cut her off completely, stopping just short of excommunication. Harbans's mother was undecided because on the one hand she wanted Harbans to be happy, but on the other, the caste-ruled community around them were appalled at this boldness which they believed would bring down the wrath of their social betters and maybe even Divine Retribution—so much so that Harbans had to move the whole family into another, more anonymous neighbourhood before they could finalise their quiet civil wedding.

But it was a match which turned out to be made in heaven. Harbans gave Sara Ann a whole new world of respect and all the pent-up adoration of a man who had been lonely for decades, which came along with a supportive freedom she had never experienced before. With her earlier life of a nun forever behind her, Sara Ann was quickly recruited in a posh English school to teach English. With a second meaningful income coming into the family, she gently pushed Harbans's mother to retire from her daily grind to a more genteel pastime of taking on sewing assignments at home—less paying but far better for her now fragile health.

With Sara Ann's support, a solid match was found for Lachhmi, the boy a respectable and soft-spoken clerk in a government office. And she supported Harbans in every way to apply for the IPS exam, which he struggled with but passed proudly on his second attempt, after which the whole family broke down in tears in front of his father's garlanded black-and-white photograph.

The respect for Harbans at work multiplied overnight, especially from the junior ranks, many of whom were from traditionally under-privileged classes in Indian society, who saw him as a role model and as a pioneer. But even though it was 1963 and the new nation of Bharat was almost two decades old, generational caste prejudices seldom fade away completely overnight. Harbans still had to complete his current duties under his current disapproving Thakur superintendent before he could be promoted into his next posting. And thus it was that when a convicted murderer escaped from Lucknow Central Jail and various routes were being assigned for the pursuers, the most tiresome and least likely one was assigned to Inspector Harbans Nat and his little team.

The wintry sun had disappeared over the horizon and a sudden hush had overtaken the world as a starry blanket of darkness fell over the earth, before they spotted the tiny railway station of Sondha.

It was little more than a whitewashed platform with a few rooms attached, with roofing which must have once been red but now appeared pink in the distance.

As they drew nearer, a tall slouching figure dressed in white came out at the sound of their engine, then disappeared back inside in a hurry, only to reappear shortly wearing a dark coat and a solar hat much favoured by colonial Englishmen.

Sewak Ram pulled the jeep up to the building in a wide sweeping flourish, to end up in a cloud of dust a few feet in front of the man standing at the entrance. Harbans hopped off and put both his hands in the small of his back as he bent backwards after the long ride, while Charan Dass uncurled himself much more slowly at the back of the jeep, straightening his rumpled uniform and putting on his cap.

The tall figure facing them was lean and somewhat stooped at the shoulders. He had a pale complexion and looked to be of indeterminate age, with a bony face and thick dark spectacle frames under the solar hat. He was wearing a black coat with the Northern Railways emblem inscribed on his breast pocket, over a white shirt and white trousers which did not look completely fresh.

Sewak Ram ratcheted up the handbrake and leaped down vigorously, saying loudly, "You there! This is ACP Harbans Nat of the Lucknow Police, you need to greet him respectfully."

Harbans sighed at Sewak Ram's overzealousness, although truth be told, he did enjoy a little bit of ceremony and he was keenly looking forward to his new title. He lifted his right hand in Sewak Ram's general direction to indicate he should hold his peace, and spoke authoritatively, "We are from the Lucknow Police department, are you the station master?"

The tall figure wrung his hands together in a nervous gesture and nodded vehemently. "I am Dhananjay Upadhyay, the station master here, sir..." he said in an unexpectedly soft, high voice.

Harbans was used to civilians being anxious in the presence of police, especially when the police appeared unannounced, so he did not read too much into Upadhyay's anxious body language—he simply nodded and looked around the sparse landscape. The station itself was a neat collection of a few whitewashed rooms with corrugated asbestos sheets with faded red paint and a long, slightly crescent-shaped concrete platform that could be seen through the entrance, with two railway lines stretching away into the distance from the platform on both sides.

"Can you confirm your identity for us?" he asked, turning back to Upadhyay.

Upadhyay nodded several times again and turned back abruptly towards the little station building, heading inwards in a long loping stride without saying a word. Harbans rolled his eyes and slowly walked in after him, gesturing for the others to follow him.

Once inside the cleanly whitewashed entrance, they were able to see the rest of the little station. It was built in a slight semicircle, as the railway line curved around it. This was peculiar, but Harbans assumed it was caused by the need to create the easiest routes for the rails through the underlying rock. There was a waiting room on the right as they entered, where they could see some old leather chairs and a table through the door. On the left was a suite of rooms marked "Station Master". The first room opened on to the platform through a huge window in addition to the door, but the second room did not appear to have any external door or window.

The platform was windswept and grey, with numbered pillars and two wooden benches which appeared to be bolted to the floor. There were a couple of stray mongrels chasing each other in the dust, while a grizzled, lean man with a turban on his head and a dirty white uniform sat on his haunches and watched them stoically.

Harbans followed Upadhyay into the Station Master's suite. The Station Master's door was at the inflexion point of the little semi-circular building, where they could see both ends of the gently curving platform. It was well furnished with a surprisingly large wooden desk and a large leather chair behind it, which had the ubiquitous white towel over the headrest to absorb perspiration. A few framed family photographs sat on the desk, along with a nameplate, an inkwell, a few cardboard-covered files and a blotter. There were two far less luxurious wooden chairs in front of the desk and a weather-beaten checked-cloth sofa in one corner, while a couple of large wardrobes took up another corner. There was a door at the back through which the other room was accessed, where Harbans could see the outlines of switching equipment and bulky telecommunications apparatus in the growing gloom.

The lights in the station master's office had already been switched on, with the harsh white glare of government-issue tube lights flooding it against the darkening skies outside. The wall behind the desk had the normal photographs of Mahatma Gandhi, Prime Minister Jawaharlal Nehru and President Dr Radhakrishnan. There was also a large portrait of Rabindranath Tagore, which Harbans found a little unusual in a government office, accompanied by a wall calendar with a colourful depiction of a Durga Puja and a small stick of incense burning on a small shelf in front of it.

Upadhyay wordlessly pointed to another of the frames hanging on the wall, without looking up to meet the Inspector's eyes. Harbans walked up to it and read the official certificate from the Railways announcing that Dhananjay Kumar Upadhyay was the station master of Sondha, along with a fuzzy black-and-white photograph that was nevertheless recognisable as the tall, spare man before him.

Upadhyay had taken off his hat and was now twisting it in his hands, looking expectantly at Harbans. He had an almost shaved head, save a little knotted lock of unshaven hair at the back of his head; this together with his name and the vermilion teeka on his forehead declared him to be a practising Brahmin.

"Hmmmm… I see," said Harbans heavily, turning away from the framed identification. "How long have you been here?"

"Erm… just over six months, sir," replied Upadhyay in his curiously soft, high voice, his head bobbing.

Being treated with this degree of obsequious respect suited Harbans, especially when the respect flowed from a member of the upper castes. He walked to the corner and sat down gingerly on the sofa, which was much more comfortable than it looked and asked in a firm voice about the train schedule for the day, which enabled Upadhyay to reconfirm their information that only one train stopped that day in Sondha, the Calcutta-bound 96 Up Sealdah Express.

Further discussions elicited that the total staffing at Sondha was the old porter whom they had seen on the platform, a maintenance engineer who visited from Lucknow twice a week and Upadhyay himself. Apparently, more than a dozen trains stopped during the rest of the week at this little tucked away station which served three different villages, all within a distance of about ten kilometres—but only one train stopped there over the current twenty-four-hour period.

Upadhyay suddenly shouted out of the window for the porter to make tea for the guests, which the old-timer would do ostensibly in the waiting room, and then seated himself with his nervous, twitchy movements.

"Sir, umm… if I may…er… ask…" he stammered hesitantly, after clearing his throat. "Why…uh, why are you asking only about the past twenty-four hours? What…what has brought you here? How am I able to… supposed to… help you with it?"

Harbans looked at the station master thoughtfully, wondering how much he should tell him. On the long trip here, he had planned to tell the whole story, but he was not sure of this odd man's reactions. As the pause stretched out into a long moment, Upadhyay shifted several times in his leather chair and went back to wringing his hands in a nervous gesture.

Harbans finally decided to be completely honest with Upadhyay. He felt he owed it to a fellow government officer, and besides, it was an issue of public safety and he did not want the station master being unprepared to defend himself, however remote the possibility.

He leaned forward and put his elbows on his knees, in a slightly melodramatic manner. "One of the most infamous murderers in memory has escaped from Lucknow Central Jail," he said portentously. "And the chief investigator suspects he may be boarding the 8 p.m. train to Sealdah tonight to get to Calcutta."

Upadhyay leaned back with a jerky move with his hands out in front of him as if to ward off some physical threat, his eyes suddenly wide behind the outsize dark spectacle frames.

Charan Dass, who was sipping his tea at the entrance, grinned and nudged Sewak Ram, who had been glaring menacingly at the dark landscape on the other side of the tracks.

"A murderer? A notorious murderer?" Upadhyay spluttered. "Why…how…what would bring him here? We are nowhere near Lucknow."

"Well, he wants to get away from Lucknow, doesn't he? No reason for him to stick close to it," remarked Harbans drily.

"But… but… why Sondha? We have nothing to help any murderers…" The Station Master had gotten up and was pacing nervously behind his outsize desk, almost speaking to himself. "If he escaped from Lucknow Central Jail, why not go to the Lucknow railway station and board any train? There are… always… there are so many trains there, day and night…"

"Well, you make a fair point," admitted Harbans, leaning back, "it is not completely certain that he is coming through here, of course. But he broke out of prison after drugging an inmate to simulate seizures, and then accompanied that inmate in the ambulance, which he hijacked after injecting the two orderlies and threatening the driver with a scalpel. It was last seen heading out of Lucknow in this general direction, so we are looking at all exit routes in this direction…"

The station master had stopped his pacing and was standing behind his desk, drinking in the details that Harbans was sharing, back to wringing his hands.

"And there is the important fact that this fugitive is a Bengali fellow called Banerjee. While his family lives in Lucknow, our intelligence tells us that he is likely to try and escape to Calcutta, which would be his best option for quickly disappearing into anonymity, where so many others look and speak like him and where so many people go and come every day." Harbans continued pensively, "And it seems to be almost too much of a coincidence that the only train which stops at Sondha today has Calcutta's bustling Sealdah station as its destination..."

Upadhyay had sat down heavily again and was muttering softly under his breath, his hands twining and intertwining repeatedly. His domed, bald head was beaded in sweat despite the chilly dusk air and he seemed a bit paler than before.

Harbans studied him quietly, feeling a little twinge of sympathy for the man's evident fear.

"Don't worry," he said brusquely, trying to be reassuring. "We are here now, he cannot get past us. And after the train departs tonight, the danger will have passed, you can go home safely. By the way," Harbans asked as a thought struck him, "how is it that you travel home? I didn't see a car or a scooter, is it parked somewhere?"

Upadhyay stopped muttering and looked up almost guiltily at Harbans, staring at him with enlarged eyes behind his thick spectacles. "I live here," he said in his soft, high voice. "My rooms are behind this on the other side of the station."

"What?" Harbans sat bolt upright. "There are other rooms behind this? Why didn't you say so in the first instance, we need to search them!" His voice rose as he spoke, his annoyance partially with himself for not having walked around the entire station earlier. "We need to see them immediately!" Harbans snapped, rising from the sofa and striding to the door.

"Yes, yes, absolutely sir… Right now, right now…" Upadhyay was clearly flustered badly by Harbans's outburst, as he awkwardly slipped on his jacket and fumbled with his solar hat.

"Come on, man, stop dithering, let's move!" Harbans chivvied him from the doorway. "I want to see the place!"

The station master walked a couple of steps towards the doorway and then turned back; he shook his head and again walked towards the doorway; yet again, he stopped abruptly, shrugged and turned and loped back to his desk.

Harbans watched this bizarre little dance of indecision with rising impatience from the platform.

"What on earth are you…?" He started to ask but was answered by a loud ringing of an electric bell on the platform as Upadhyay pressed a button on a console next to his desk.

The station master hurried out, smiling weakly at Harbans's sour expression. "It is our protocol," he offered as an explanation. "The station master has to let the staff know when he is absenting himself from his official post…"

Harbans snorted in derision, looking pointedly at the elderly porter who was back on his haunches, his hands warming themselves around an earthenware cup of tea. "What protocol? There is one lonely old porter who you can easily tell on the way out!" He barked irritably, but the eccentric station master had already vanished through the entrance with his long loping walk.

Harbans snapped his fingers at Sewak Ram and Charan Dass to walk behind him as he followed Upadhyay, who loped around the corner of the building to a little two-roomed structure that was hidden behind the curve of the station building. It had an electric street lamp lighting up the façade and a tiny little white-fenced garden with a rich profusion of colourful flowers growing in well-manicured bushes, in front of neatly whitewashed walls with a dark wooden door and shuttered windows.

The station master stopped outside the gate in the fence and pointed at the door. "Why don't you… If you can please…" He stammered.

"Where's the key?" Harbans asked, treading carefully through the gate. He had a sixth sense about these situations which had normally served him well in the past and he was feeling distinctly edgy now.

"It's never locked," replied Upadhyay quickly, in his soft high voice.

Harbans signalled with his left hand to Sewak Ram to guard the window and Charan Dass to follow him. He felt the hairs on the nape of his neck rise as he unbuckled his revolver with his right hand and stepped into the darkened little house in a swift, easy motion.

The light from the open doorway spilled into the front room and threw shifting shadows across the floor and onto the opposite wall. It was packed with ancient, overstuffed furniture—but it was empty.

"Come on in, there is no one here," Harbans called out.

Upadhyay came in slowly and flicked on a light switch. Another government-issue tube light came on, flooding the room with harsh white light.

"Umm… there are… there are… more rooms," Upadhyay said in an unsteady voice, holding back at the doorway.

They went through the rest of the house together, the tiny little sleeping quarter with clothes strewn untidily all over, the sparse kitchenette and the sizeable bathroom, which was littered with little tufts of hair and a carelessly discarded razor that explained the station master's freshly shaven head.

All of it was calmly devoid of runaway convicts.

Harbans felt the tension in his shoulders relax as he holstered his revolver. He felt a little silly for his unwarranted concern and cursed the dark, deserted isolation of the place for winding him up.

"All clear, no problems," he announced to no one in particular. "Now we just have to guard the station and prevent that damn convict from boarding…"

"Actually, sir…" began Upadhyay softly.

"What now? Is there another hidden mansion we should know about?" Harbans asked with a heavy attempt at sarcasm.

"Well, the station is bent, you know…" Upadhyay drew a crescent in the air with his hands. "And we cannot see one end of the station from the other. But the train slows down while approaching the station and is also slowly gaining speed when leaving it, so if we want to catch anyone jumping on board, we must guard the approach to the station and the exit from it… both sides…" he finished hesitantly.

Harbans realised the station master had a valid point even before he had finished speaking. He looked out into the darkness and cursed again, fluently and long, while his constables hefted their guns uncomfortably. This was going to be a tough job for only three men, if indeed the convict Banerjee was going to jump on the train in the darkness around the station.

"All right, all right—we need to disperse, I will take the platform!" He barked, assigning Sewak Ram and Charan Dass to opposite ends of the platform to peer into the darkness.

Harbans gloomily watched the constables go their way and felt around in his pocket for his crumpled pack of cigarettes.

"Are you coming?" He asked Upadhyay, who had oddly chosen this moment to gather and fold his scattered clothes to stack them back in the little cupboard.

"Why did he spare the orderlies and the driver?" Upadhyay suddenly asked in his soft high voice.

"What?" Harbans said, caught by surprise.

Upadhyay had been leaning over his bed folding clothes, and he now stretched upright. "Well, you said, sir, that he had drugged some people and then threatened someone else with a scalpel—but he did not kill anyone while escaping. Sorry to suggest… But … You know…It does not sound like a vicious murderer, more like a thinking person with a plan…"

The inspector's brow furrowed in thought as he bent his head to light up his cigarette, throwing the used match out of the window.

"Well, he was not the average criminal, you know," Harbans began pensively. "As I remember from the file, he was a first-year student at Lucknow Medical College when he was arrested…"

The station master had stopped his chores and was standing still with a half-folded shirt in his hands, listening intently to Harbans.

"It was an unusual case, it made headlines across the country almost a decade ago," the inspector continued, blowing out a stream of blue smoke to add to the dark air of the night.

"There are all sorts of extreme ragging activities in residential medical colleges, not that I fully understand them." Harbans leaned against the door jamb and spoke in between drags of the cigarette, recalling the details. "In this case, there was apparently a student who was not comfortable with dissection and blood, who was also a bit shy and introverted. I guess he made himself a bit of a target amongst the other students.

"Well, one winter evening, his batchmates decided to have a grisly bit of fun with him. They darkened the floor of the hostel where his rooms were and they borrowed the still bleeding severed legs of an accident victim from the hospital morgue and put it under his covers for him to find when he returned from dinner. Then they waited together around the corner for him to discover the macabre surprise.

"So it happened that, after dinner that night, the young man duly went back to his room, no doubt taken aback by the darkness all over the rest of the floor. His batchmates were gathered in a group around the corner, waiting for the moment of discovery, listening for a scream or a yell—but there was no sound for a while.

"After a while of straining their ears, the gathered batchmates were taken aback to hear a low, throaty chuckling coming from the room…"

Harbans stopped for a moment, the end of his cigarette glowing red as he took a long, deep drag.

Upadhyay was standing upright with the half-folded shirt hanging limply from his hands, an intensely expectant look on his face.

"They listened for a moment, unable to discern what had happened. Then they crept forward slowly together to peer around the corner, where a dreadful, chilling sight met their eyes.

"Their shy, introverted batchmate was sitting cross-legged on his bed, one of the severed legs on his lap, tearing strips off the other one with his teeth. He was covered in drying blood, his face and hands had strips of the dead man's flesh all over them, while he was smiling intermittently and mumbling incoherently to himself. Their prank had driven him over the edge of madness."

Upadhyay exhaled sharply as if he had been punched in the stomach. "This was so… so cruel. Horrible, horrible," he said with a great deal of feeling. "And so needless… why?…why?"

Harbans shook his head. "Honestly, I have no idea why they did this. But I have seen in my job that people are capable of immense thoughtless cruelty, especially in a large group where no one has to take individual accountability. Anyhow, that was not the story of our murderer. That story comes now." The dapper little inspector continued, "The introverted, unfortunate young man had a brother in the same medical college, apparently a much stronger person. This brother happened to come visiting while the group was staring at the horrific tableau of madness and he was completely distraught at the sight. Then, as he realised what had been done to his brother, he grabbed one of the severed legs in a fit of blind anger and attacked the group of students with it, his strength fed manifold by his anguished rage.

"Such was his frenzy that even a group of almost a dozen students could not contain him. The commotion immediately attracted a number of other students and a couple of watchmen, who helped to quell him and hold him down—but by that time, the damage was done. One of the pranksters had been pierced through the eye with a femur, that is the thigh bone, from the severed leg. And another had his carotid artery slashed by a shard of sawed off bone. Both students succumbed to their injuries, despite being in the premises of a medical college hospital."

"But why… why was he treated like a murderer?" The station master seemed genuinely perplexed. "He was only… he was protecting his brother…?"

"Come on, don't be naïve." Harbans's response was sharp; as a member of the law enforcement forces, he felt annoyed by the man's reaction. "The damage was already done to his crazy brother, the time for defence was well past. It was just a violent act of revenge—which is how the courts saw it too. Plus, here was an upper-caste family, while both victims were lower-caste students who had been admitted on a reserved quota. With all the complications, the killer Banerjee got a double life sentence, which means he will never walk free in his lifetime."

Upadhyay seemed a bit chastened by the inspector's admonishment, then he wanted to know, "Do you know what happened to the other brother?"

"There is no further record of him." Harbans shrugged his indifference, finished his cigarette and flicked it out of the window, blowing out more smoke. "I need some tea, are you coming?" He asked.

Upadhyay had slumped on the bed and was staring ahead sightlessly.

"Come on, we have to get back," Harbans said again, more authoritatively. "I need some tea!"

Upadhyay shook himself from his reverie and looked up at the inspector, his enlarged eyes behind his spectacles revealing how disturbed he was by the story. "I am coming, I want to… I will just finish…" He pointed at the remaining clothes lying on the bed.

After his initial obsequious behaviour, this sudden intransigence was somewhat unexpected for Harbans, who gave him a long hard look, but the strange fellow had already gone back to folding his clothes again; the mundane chore appeared to be his coping mechanism. The inspector gave a small, annoyed shake of his head and walked out into the chilly night air, where he looked up at the starry night sky, much clearer here than it was in the city.

He stood there for a few moments, wondering if the escaped fugitive was lurking in the bushes around the station, possibly freezing without adequate protective clothing. His sixth sense was prickling him again, but he could find no logical reason to believe that the convict Banerjee had come this far to jump on a train. He stamped his feet and blew on his hands as the night cold crept up on him, calling out loudly to Charan Dass and Sewak Ram to see if they were in position. Both replied confidently from a distance, which gave him some encouragement as he walked back into the station.

To his utter surprise, Upadhyay was leaning back in his chair in the Station Master's office, reading one of the cardboard-covered files.

"How did you get in here? I didn't see you come past me!" Harbans demanded to know.

Upadhyay had jumped to his feet when the Inspector entered. "Oh, there is a back way from the station into the quarters," he said, motioning the inspector politely to a chair.

Harbans walked pointedly to the sofa, away from the chair, and asked irritably, "If there is a back way, why didn't you take us through it in the first place?"

"It was locked from the inside, Inspector saab. Otherwise, of course, I would have taken you through that way, why wouldn't I?" Upadhyay spoke in a conciliatory tone, sitting down again.

Harbans realised the station master was right, but he felt annoyed nevertheless. He thought this man was really strange and he figured this was the reason why an upper-caste government servant was posted in the solitary wilderness, not a posting that anyone would have normally volunteered for.

"Where is the tea?" Harbans snapped, trying to re-establish his control over the situation.

The station master looked blank for a moment and then jumped up and walked to the door. "I will make it for you," he said. "That old porter is useless."

He was back in a few minutes with two earthen cups of steaming tea and a paper plate with two tired-looking samosas, to find Harbans writing up his report in his government-issue notebook.

Harbans waved the samosas away and grimaced as he took his first sip of the tea, which was sickly sweet. Nevertheless, he continued sipping the milky brown liquid, which was warming in the chilly night air, as he continued writing up his notes in silence.

Upadhyay went into the adjoining room and emerged with green, red and white flags in his hands. "It is almost time, sir. I will head out to the station to signal the train," he said. "You will soon hear the train whistle."

Harbans felt a flood of adrenaline surge through him—it was time.

He bustled out of the door and strode to both ends of the station, calling out again to Charan Dass and Sewak Ram, both of whom reconfirmed they were in position. The inspector realised this might alert the escaped convict if he was hiding there, but his main objective was to prevent any escape.

He went back to the Station Master's doorway, from where he could see both ends of the curving platform, and took up a watchful position there, his hand on his holster, trying to shake off a sudden tiredness in his limbs.

They did not have long to wait. They heard the plaintive whistle of the 96 Up Sealdah Express as it swept towards the station, slowing down as it got nearer. Then the smoking engine emerged eerily out of the darkness, hissing and steaming loudly, followed by carriages with cheerful lighted windows showing a range of humanity travelling inside.

Harbans craned his neck to look at both sides of the station, his eyelids inexplicably heavy, his breath increasingly shallow.

As he turned heavily right towards the engine, he saw the station master walk towards it with confident strides, exchanging pleasantries and laughing with the engine drivers as he jumped in with them.

He turned to the left as the train began to depart slowly after its brief stop and he saw the station master with his long loping stride reach the guard's cabin at the rear and pull himself in with the guard's help.

He staggered in surprise and tried to shout, but his throat was suddenly constricted and he fell awkwardly sideways on the desk, bringing down the files and photographs with him as he tumbled to the floor. He scrabbled uselessly for his holster, but his arms refused to follow his will.

He turned his head helplessly as the train puffed its way slowly out of the station and his eyes fell on a sepia-tinted framed photograph lying on the floor next to him, which showed two young twin boys with their parents in front of the Bara Imambara in Lucknow.

And he suddenly understood where the other brother was.

9

The SMS Murder

The first SMS, which performed the miraculous task of converting an incidental death into a wilful murder, announced itself with a loud ping during the morning briefing on 11 October, two days after Kali Puja and Diwali.

Assistant Commissioner of Police Pradyot Banerjee heard his phone inform him of the arrival of the message, but made a calibrated decision not to look at it immediately. He was conscious that he had recently taken over his command as a fresh IPS officer a bare three months ago and was still establishing credibility with his team of hardened, professional police officers in the most high-profile fresh IPS posting in Kolkata—assistant commissioner of police in homicide investigations, under the joint commissioner of crime in the Detective Department.

No matter the temptation, he knew he had to stay focused on the briefing.

While the city was still slowly recovering from the extended festivities of Kali Puja and Diwali and while the general populace reluctantly made peace with the commercial reality of getting back to work, the grisly business of unnatural death had nevertheless continued unabated.

A drunken brawl between European backpacker tourists and a local gang in Chitpur had led to the death of a young German. An Odia working man had had his head smashed in on the riverfront, ostensibly for his Puja bonus that had been ripped out of his pocket. A Chinese restaurateur had been shot dead in his home above the restaurant in Tangra, the erstwhile tannery part of Kolkata which was home to the Chinese community. A housewife had succumbed to her injuries after being brutally beaten and robbed in her home by an intruder. And a pavement dweller's body had been inexplicably found inside the branch of an international bank when they opened after the holidays.

There was a plethora of plausible suspects in each case; all the forensic updates were duly shared and the investigation activities were meticulously recorded during the meeting, with investigating officers taking the opportunity to offer suggestions and insights to each other—a collaborative aspect of the Kolkata Police that Pradyot was proud of.

After all the discussions were over and the actions for the day agreed, Pradyot dismissed the group and as they all hurried off to their day's tasks, Pradyot took out his phone to read the text message, walking back to his office with his characteristic long strides.

"Get an autopsy done for the death in suite 11008," it said.

Pradyot slowed down as he absorbed the message. There was no clue as to who had sent it, the number was blocked which in itself was a puzzle since the telecom companies in India did not offer number blocking as a service due to the government guidelines—although he knew that a few powerful people did have blocked telephone numbers.

But more to the point—what did it mean? And why was it sent to him?

"Kundu!" He called out as he entered his room and sat down.

His aide, Inspector Kundu, entered practically on his heels and saluted. A dark, spare man with a cheerful countenance and twinkling eyes, he was a two-decade-old veteran of the force, having climbed quickly through the ranks through dogged tenacity and a punishing work ethic.

Pradyot waved at his own forehead in a casual return salute and showed Inspector Kundu the SMS message. As Kundu wrinkled his forehead over it, Pradyot bent over his desk and dialled the Kolkata Police Control Room.

"Control Room, Constable Maya Sharma," came a crisp response.

Pradyot was acquainted with Maya and greeted her comfortably, then asked about any recently reported death involving a suite 11008.

There was a brief pause, presumably as Maya searched the database, then she answered in Bengali, "Sir, industrialist Krishna Kumar Bagla died in room 11008 of the Taj Bengal hotel overnight."

This came as quite a surprise since the deceased was a prominent local industrialist, but the death had not been reported in the media as yet. Pradyot was immediately suspicious—the mysterious SMS sender was apparently talking about a real death that was not yet public… He took a moment to absorb the information and then asked, "What did he die of? Was there an autopsy?"

This time there was an even longer pause, and then Maya responded, "He died of a heart attack, Sir, confirmed by a medical examination. There was no need for an autopsy."

Pradyot chewed his lower lip thoughtfully while Constable Maya waited and then finally asked, "Who is the Medical Examiner in this case please, Maya?"

"Dr Sushmita Sinha," she replied.

Pradyot thanked her and hung up, then asked the operator to connect him to Dr Sinha. As he waited for the call, he sent Inspector Kundu off to get in touch with the telecom company and identify the sender of the SMS.

The phone on his desk rang again. It was the operator connecting him to Dr Sinha.

"Hello?" A deep, rich female voice spoke.

Pradyot introduced himself and then asked about the death in suite 11008. "Are you sure it was a heart attack?"

Dr Sinha sounded firm but cautious. "Look, ACP Banerjee, we have never met so I cannot identify your voice. Do you mind if I call back on the official Police Headquarters line and ask to be reconnected to you before discussing the case in hand?"

Pradyot readily agreed and within a minute, they were speaking again.

"Is there a problem?" Dr Sinha's first question.

"I don't know as yet, just checking the circumstances," Pradyot reassured her as truthfully as possible.

"Well, the swift examination I did showed all the symptoms consistent with a heart attack," said Dr Sinha.

Pradyot's interest was piqued. "Why swift?" He asked.

Dr Sinha took her time, obviously choosing her words carefully, "I understand it was very sensitive for the hotel… and his sons were also present by that time… they wanted to resolve the matter quickly."

Pradyot sensed some doubt in her tone and jumped in quickly, "So, do you think an autopsy might in fact be called for? Where is the body? Can it be done?"

Dr Sinha took even longer to answer, somewhat hesitantly this time. "There was some discolouration of his hands which I would have liked to investigate further… but the family may not agree to any further examination of the body… it is likely they will cremate him before anything can be done…"

"Is there nothing that can be done?" Pradyot interjected quickly again.

It seemed that Dr Sinha had thought through some options herself. "Well, as a shortcut of sorts, I do have a sample of the stomach contents which we pumped out as he had vomited slightly. And his blood reports—I can rush through a preliminary report if you need it."

"Oh thanks, that would be great. Please, can you do it urgently?" Pradyot asked. "If it shows anything significant, we need to get to the family before the cremation."

Dr Sinha agreed and hung up.

Pradyot busied himself in the mountain of paperwork that inevitably piled up on his desk and demanded his attention, no matter how often and how rigorously he attacked it. Interdepartmental briefings, new training material, requests for equipment, closure notes for old files all demanded his attention and he thought no more of the mysterious SMS for the next hour.

But Dr Sinha's return call dragged his attention back to the mysterious SMS.

"I am afraid it's serious," she immediately started without introduction. "It looks like a planned death, not a natural one."

"Really? So then how was the first diagnosis…?" Pradyot started, before she blurted out, "It is a poison called aconite that I have not experienced since my training days. From a plant commonly known as wolfsbane. A large quantity had been wiped on his hands, which simulated symptoms similar to heart attack and caused his death.

"It is very easy to mistake the outcome as a heart attack, especially if the patient is dead and cannot describe the symptoms," she continued, obviously keen to explain how and why the diagnosis had changed.

She continued with more technical details, but Pradyot's mind was moving on to the various actions that he had to take. He knocked on the glass panel of his room and signalled for Kundu to come in. He waited for Dr Sinha's explanation to end and asked her to immediately advise the family, the hotel and the overseeing officer from the Kolkata Police. She replied a little tartly that she was well aware of her responsibilities and was informing him first out of courtesy. As soon as he could mollify and thank her and hang up, he asked Kundu to get the Alipore police station in-charge and Detective Inspector Bagchi to the scene immediately to commence investigations. He would meet them there.

Pradyot strode out of his office and made his way to the bank of elevators. As he hurried through the office, a number of people returned the tall young man's smile and greeted him cheerfully. He took the elevator to the top floor and made his way to the suite of offices of Sikander Azizi, JPC Crime, where he asked the very formal secretary that he needed to meet the JPC immediately on a confidential matter.

This was an unusual request, but she rang through to ask Azizi.

Pradyot came from one of the most influential families in Kolkata, although he wore this social pedigree with ease and charm. His grandfather had been a cabinet minister in the Congress regime in the 1970s and the wealthy transportation family had thrived under successive regimes as well, with his father having served as Mayor of Kolkata earlier and currently serving as an influential Member of the State Legislative Assembly. Pradyot tried to not leverage this heritage in his day-to-day life, but today was a special occasion.

A group of officers exited Azizi's office and greeted him with looks of curiosity as Azizi came to the door and ushered him in. Pradyot waited till the grey-haired, heavily built Azizi closed the door and then embarked on a full disclosure of the events of the morning on the Bagla case. Azizi's normal intense expression turned even more forbidding as he continued. By the time Pradyot finished, Azizi was scowling heavily as he cracked his knuckles.

"This is going to be very sensitive, very sensitive indeed," he rasped in his gravelly voice. "They are a well-known business family and to find their patriarch murdered in a hotel… All the indications are that it will turn nasty.

"I will inform the commissioner and we'll use the PR office to keep the press at bay for the moment. You must always be very careful when dealing with the family, no accusations or arrests or any sudden action until we have every piece of evidence tied up and discussed with me—understand, son?"

After going through a few other details on the officers assigned to the case, Azizi patted Pradyot on his back and sent him on his way.

Half an hour later, the white police Mahindra XUV assigned to ACP Banerjee pulled up at the imposing porch of the Taj Bengal hotel.

The hotel lobby was as busy as usual, but the general manager of the hotel, Rajeev Bagga, had been alerted and was waiting for him in the lobby, along with his senior team. He led Pradyot quickly through the lobby elevators to the eleventh floor and down the corridor to the spacious suite 11008, which had been turned into a full-fledged crime scene with the forensics team in gloves and paper shoe covers going through the entire room.

Detective Inspector Bagchi was in charge on the ground, his men had used their time well to interview all the staff who had been in contact with the deceased.

The hotel service team had a sordid tale to tell.

Mr Bagla had a standing suite in his name in the hotel, which was paid for in advance every few months in cash. It was informally well known that Mr Bagla had young women supplied to him in that room, where he entertained them with other senior political and business connections. Drinks flowed to that room and the billing was high, and sometimes the hotel staff had even been asked to quietly escort some hurt or dazed young women out through back entrances. The women never pressed charges and neither did the 'friends' who accompanied them.

Since Mr Bagla was a known contributor to the Chief Minister's election and was one of the industrialists who had the CM's confidence in rebuilding business in Bengal, besides also being frequently pictured in the newspapers with senior police officials, the hotel management only registered these goings-on discreetly with their police contact to cover themselves but never lodged any formal complaint.

Apparently, the night of 10 October had been one such night. Mr Bagla had been alone and a couple of young women had kept him company—a young Russian lady from out of town and a local girl. The team of detectives had tracked them down and were bringing them in.

Pradyot reminded Inspector Kundu to chase the telecom company about the source of the SMS and then looked over the interview details garnered by the detective team. Nobody had seen Mr Bagla after 8 p.m. the previous night, nor had there been any housekeeping or room service requests from the room. When repeated knocking this morning elicited no response, the housekeeping staff entered to find him dead in his bed.

Pradyot asked Detective Inspector Bagchi to check the closed circuit TV images around the hotel and also interview the neighbouring room residents, firmly overriding the objections of the hotel management. He quickly answered a few text messages from his friends planning to catch up at bar night in Saturday Club and one from his mother asking about dinner and then left with Inspector Kundu to interview the family, Kundu calling ahead to let them know that the ACP and he were on their way. Given the sensitivity of the case and the Bagla family's position, he was well aware that this was something he could not delegate to other members of the investigative team.

Despite the foreknowledge, their car waited outside the gates of the palatial mansion in Alipore for almost ten minutes. Kundu too had the opportunity to update him that the SMS in the morning had come from a Dubai-based mobile number, roaming in India that morning. Kolkata Police had asked the Dubai police authorities to help identify the owner of the connection, but there was no information yet, which only helped deepen the mystery. The police driver punched the horn impatiently and the gates opened at last, leading them through the sweeping gravel driveway past manicured lawns to the main house.

The family had all gathered in the main drawing room—the frail Mrs Bagla in her early sixties, her three sons, two daughters-in-law and four grandchildren, one of them a toddler.

Pradyot offered his condolences gently and was met with a sulky, stony silence and hostile unblinking eyes. He groaned inwardly as he was made aware that he had disrupted the mourning family during lunch, the first meal they were eating since they had been informed of the demise of the head of their family, then began the tedious but necessary task of going through the various standard questions with each member of the family.

After almost two hours of relentless questioning over a cup of tea and assorted savoury snacks that were the trademark of traditional Marwari hospitality even in a time of great stress, he had to admit there did not seem any likely clues here.

Mrs Bagla spoke no English and only a smattering of Bengali and was extremely aggressive in a rough Bihari dialect, reminding him that Krishna Kumar Bagla had come up the hard way through the mining mafia in Bihar and Bengal, with rumours of his disposing of opponents personally with country made revolvers in his early days. The two elder sons were made in the image of their father, tough businessmen who answered only what they had to. The youngest son had a glazed expression and an apparent inability to comprehend the questions which his mother said was caused by grief, but which Pradyot strongly suspected was due to protracted substance abuse. And the wives were as frightened as the children.

The upshot was that Krishna Kumar Bagla had been an unquestionable force in his own household and no one in the family seemed to know what he had been doing or where he was the previous evening.

When asked if he had any enemies who wanted him dead, they all steadfastly upheld in their own different ways that he was a good man who made no enemies. This was very surprising, given the many public business rivalries that the Bagla family had generated, including the most recent spat with his cousin, Sushant Kumar Bagla, over control of their bauxite and aluminium business. Pradyot guessed they had all discussed it in advance and deliberately chosen to be ultra-cautious, so as not to proactively offer up any line of investigation where some details known to the deceased but not to the family could backfire on them.

Worried about not making progress, he nevertheless thanked them and rose. Inspector Kundu left both their cards with the contact details as he made his way out to the car, dialling Azizi to report the day's proceedings.

Azizi listened intently, asking him to repeat himself a couple of times as incoming text messages on Pradyot's phone interrupted the signal. As he finished, Azizi's gravelly voice growled at him through the telephone, "We really cannot open up a can of worms by implicating a wider business community in the investigation. So far, the media channels and sites have only covered it as the death of a prominent businessman, without details. Kolkata cannot afford to have this huge negative scandal—try any other tack of investigation, son, let's find someone we can prosecute without any political complications."

Pradyot clenched his teeth in frustration, thinking to himself—*I cannot manufacture a convenient murderer, I have to follow the evidence. What is the old man thinking? Really!*

But he said, "I understand, all our efforts will be focused in that direction, sir," before hanging up.

He leaned back in his seat and then recalled the incoming SMS's, expecting more reminders from his friends. But as he swiped his smartphone, his long day of disappointment so far was suddenly wiped away and his pulse quickened.

"Check under the front seat of his car," said the first message from a private number.

"Look in the safe in room 802," immediately after that.

They were pulling into the driveway of the Taj Bengal hotel by that time. Pradyot despatched Kundu to oversee a search of the car, which K.K. Bagla had been driving himself the previous night. Apparently, a driver had come around at daybreak but had not taken the car, which had been impounded by the police later that morning. Pradyot himself hurried in and asked to see the general manager again, making a quick call to ask the forensics team from suite 11008 to return to the hotel to search through the car.

It transpired that room 802 was in the name of Daniel Hong, a prominent Chinese restaurateur. This struck Pradyot as odd, why would Mr Hong book a room in the hotel if he lived in the same city? Did Mr Hong practise the same discreet extracurricular activities as Mr Bagla?

The front office staff all recalled Mr Hong leaving in the morning. Calls to his room and to his mobile phone elicited no response, so the housekeeping staff was called in to open the room to the police.

Meanwhile, Detective Inspector Bagchi reported that the preliminary viewing of the CCTV recordings had thrown up a few suspicious interactions between Mr Bagla and other guests—one in particular where the guest had been shaking hands with him in the elevator lobby just before he went to his room. The two working girls had nothing to add, except that Mr Bagla let them go in a few minutes as he was feeling unwell.

Room 802 was normal and quite unremarkable at first sight. Since there was no cause for suspicion other than an anonymous SMS, Pradyot was reluctant to let the forensics team commence digging around. He was wondering whether he could impose on the hotel to open the safe without a warrant, when he saw that the safe door was already ajar.

Inside was a two-page handwritten note, addressed to the police, and a pair of soft leather gloves.

Pradyot read through the letter quickly and slowly once again, his rising disbelief showing in the expression on his face. He wandered over to the sofa next to the window and sat down heavily, to read the letter slowly again, more thoroughly. Then he leaned back for a long moment, looking out of the window with unseeing eyes as his mind grappled with the flurry of shocking new information.

After a few minutes of considering the various emerging scenarios, he shook himself out of his reverie and abruptly ordered the forensics team, who had been waiting patiently outside, to commence a sweep of the room. Pradyot also clicked a photo of the letter with his phone and sent it to JPC Azizi. He then handed over command of the site to Detective Inspector Bagchi, with strict instructions to the hotel management to keep it sealed off, while he headed downstairs.

Inspector Kundu met him as he was walking out of the elevator. Kundu had an air of momentous importance about him as he drew Pradyot into a corner and updated him in a stage whisper that they had found a gun, 0.22 calibre, wrapped in an oilcloth under the front passenger seat of the Jaguar XJL that Mr Bagla had been driving. Pradyot looked up sharply at Kundu's excited face, confirmed with the inspector it had been sent for ballistic testing and fingerprints and then called for his car.

"Chinatown," he barked at the driver as he and Inspector Kundu climbed in. "Put on the siren and make it quick!"

It was past 5 p.m. by now, the sun was setting as they drove over the longest flyover in the city and turned around at the EM Bypass and into Tangra, the erstwhile tannery area, where the Chinese community in Kolkata had long traditionally lived. The core of the construction in the area was almost two hundred years old, on which several new, very often mismatched layers had been built by succeeding generations. The narrow roads and forbidding walls of the overseeing buildings spoke of a more secretive, private and inhibited bygone era.

As they drove through, it seemed that a myriad lanes furtively snaked away from the street-lit central road into the surrounding gloom as if to escape their attention. They passed the glittering Chinese restaurants which were now the mainstay of the community, still festooned with Diwali decorations, and went deeper into the heart of Tangra towards the address that was their destination.

Kundu had called ahead, so Detective Inspector Bharat Kumar, who was overseeing the Chinese restaurant murder, met them at the entrance to the Joyous Dragon. It was an old building from the colonial days, with a new and imposing façade with faux arches and pillars that looked what it was—a somewhat fine-dining eatery pitched at a much more exclusive clientele. The ground and first floors had been converted into impressive upmarket dining spaces, with a number of discreet wood-panelled party rooms on the second floor. Pradyot had never been there before, but he was well aware of its recent popularity and he took in the highlights of the clearly successful eatery as they climbed the stairs to the family abode on the third floor.

Pradyot recalled the key details of the case from the previous day's briefing.

Bernard 'Bonny' Lim had been born and raised in Tangra in the late 1970s and 1980s. He had a wild history of vicious street gang activity, peddling drugs to wealthy students, even being expelled from school during his childhood. In his late teens, he had run away on a cargo ship bound for Hong Kong, where he had apparently prospered for some time surprisingly as a commodities trader. After a decade he had called his elder brother Tony to join him with Tony's family and after his father passed away, his mother Joyce as well.

In the new millennium, Bonny Lim had shifted away from Hong Kong amidst fragmented news filtering back of trouble with the Triads, who still ruled the streets of the city after the British handover. He had reportedly moved unobtrusively to Singapore and then just as quietly to Sydney before suddenly showing up back in Tangra less than a decade ago with suitcases full of cash, and his mother Joyce. He had taken his time to survey the business landscape before going into partnership with one of the foremost local Tangra restaurateurs to build the Joyous Dragon into a major force. He had built a strong position in the community and with his partner and had even married the man's divorced daughter Allie, while adopting and giving a home to Allie's daughter Linda from her previous marriage to an Anglo-Indian marine captain.

In the early evening of Diwali, two nights ago, when the restaurant was bustling with wealthy clientele at all levels, Bonny Lim had been shot dead with a small-calibre gun in the corridor outside his bedroom in his apartment. His wife had been next door with her father, the three domestic servants had gone down to help with Diwali rush, his stepdaughter Linda had been asleep in her room and had only heard the fireworks outside (and probably mistaken the gunshots to be firecrackers) and his mother Joyce was too deaf to have heard the shots. His body was discovered by one of the domestic servants, who had finished helping out at the restaurant and had come home to find him sprawled in his own blood in the corridor between his own and Linda's bedroom, shot multiple times in his face.

The ongoing police investigation had thrown up a number of people with a grudge against Bonny Lim. It seemed that under the veneer of the successful upstanding citizen, Bonny Lim had continued to be an unpleasant, self-serving and untrustworthy character—as testified to by sacked ex-employees, a very disgruntled supplier, the neighbours with whom there was a land dispute and a city property developer who alleged financial malfeasance.

Bonny Lim's widow Allie inherited his considerable wealth, and since in over 70 per cent of residential murders the culprit was found to be the spouse, she was immediately scrutinised as a prime suspect despite her alibi, which was being challenged in any case since it was provided by her father. The Kolkata Police were also waiting upon reports from Hong Kong, Singapore and Sydney, which could throw up further leads.

But Pradyot was here for another reason.

Bonny Lim's partner and his father-in-law was Daniel Hong of room 802.

Pradyot stooped to get through the low doorway and stepped gently into the living quarters of the family on the third floor. He looked around and instinctively hunched his shoulders, feeling a bit cramped for room. The living quarters seemed to be made of predominantly wooden walls, breaking up the larger spaces into tiny rooms opening into each other, most of them painted in dull, dark shades with scenes from China painted directly on the walls. The sense of closed spaces was exacerbated by hanging lamps with low-watt bulbs covered by dark Chinese silk shades. The overall impression was a bit smoky and exotic, like a long-kept secret.

The barefoot Chinese servant who opened the door led them silently into a sitting area, where they stood around until Joyce Lim entered on a wheelchair. She was wearing traditional Chinese mourning clothes and her wrinkled face was ravaged with grief, with eyes that looked like they had shed every possible tear.

"Again and again you come, what you wan' from us? Jus' go and fin' out who kill my Bonny…!' She burst out hoarsely as Pradyot started to offer his condolences.

A petite, middle-aged woman with long dark hair came into the room and quickly bent over Joyce, saying, "Hush Mama, they are doing their job", followed by a few words in Cantonese. She was wearing a dark knee-length dress and a full-sleeved jacket over it with the collar turned up, which was buttoned up to the top of her neck despite the humid autumn evening. Pradyot noticed the thick, heavy spectacle frames she wore because she kept adjusting them with both hands, as if they were new.

She introduced herself in a soft voice as Allie Lim and Pradyot offered his condolences again, which were accepted dully, though courteously, by her.

Two children had followed Allie into the room.

Linda, the elder, was a petite teenager with her mother's long dark hair who clutched her mother obsessively, shrinking behind her with tearful eyes whenever Pradyot or Kundu ventured a question about her father. She seemed like a tiny, frightened helpless animal and reminded Pradyot of someone he had met, but he could not put his finger on it.

The boy was barely five, he did not really seem to understand what was happening as he alternated between pugnacious showing off and petulant whining. Pradyot had seen this kind of erratic behaviour before in children who were dealing with sudden death without adequate adult support, so he did not question the child at all.

For the next couple of hours, Pradyot and Kundu once again went over the testimony of each of the people who had been interviewed earlier, armed with the new information from the letter in room 802.

Apparently, Bonny Lim had left the restaurant on Diwali night to go to the living quarters for some reason. No one had seen him go. No one else was in the apartment other than Linda and Joyce, both of whom were asleep. None of the restaurant staff went to the living quarters and the domestic only returned to find Bonny's body.

The investigating officer Kumar and his team had already established a timeline chart and had cross-checked all alibis, which had all held up.

With key members of the staff standing respectfully in front of them, Pradyot sat back from the sheaf of papers spread out on a table in front of him and asked thoughtfully, "Was Mr Krishna Kumar Bagla there that night?"

The restaurant manager answered immediately, without hesitation, "Yes sir, he had a private party in his booth", then gazed at Pradyot with curious eyes, clearly looking for further information. Further probing revealed that Mr Bagla was hosting a party of senior gentlemen, many of whom went to and from the luxury toilet on the second floor during the course of the evening.

While no one had been seen going up the stairs to the private apartment, it was quite clear that there was enough opportunity that evening to slip up unnoticed.

Pradyot left his team there to ensure that all details had been recorded and all interviewees had signed their statements and took his leave of the mourning family, none of whom seemed to register it given the continuing police activity in their private space.

It was almost 8 p.m. by now. Once in the car, Pradyot called JPC Azizi again to update him. Azizi's gravelly voice on the phone sounded tense and Pradyot was not surprised to be called into the police headquarters for a full debrief.

Tired though he was, he swiped his phone to the photograph of the sensational letter from the safe in room 802, reading through the bizarre and terrible contents once again, still surprised by it. Written in a terse and staccato manner, the narrative style was in sharp contrast to the sensational contents:

To the Police Commissioner
Kolkata Police
11 October

My name is Daniel Hong. I am handwriting this confession in full possession of my faculties.

Krishna Kumar Bagla and I were mere acquaintances until we had an enforced layover together in London Heathrow for a twenty-hour period a month ago. He became deeply inebriated on that occasion and confessed he desperately wanted his cousin and competitor Sushant Bagla dead. I was drunk as well and also expressed a wish for my son-in-law Bonny Lim to die.

In our drunken state, we explored the idea of each committing the murder for the other—something he said he had read in a book. That way, there would be no apparent motive connecting him to the death of my enemy or me to the death of his.

We did not give up the idea once we returned to Kolkata and we spoke once more to finalise the first death.

On Diwali on 10 October, Bagla hosted evening drinks in a private room at our restaurant.

I had asked Bonny to be in their living quarters at 6 p.m. for a meeting with me.

Bagla went up the stairs when the staff were occupied, and shot Bonny with an untraceable gun he had acquired during his travels in the Bihar mining districts.

After the event I was deeply shocked at how my daughter and her children broke down and indeed at my own sudden revulsion at my actions and for conspiring with Bagla.

I resolved to end this murder pact without further killing of innocents, but Bagla was absolutely adamant. Seeing his attitude I felt that he was the real evil in this situation and I resolved to end the matter with his death.

I then arranged for him to have a rendezvous with overseas prostitutes in Taj Bengal in his usual suite, paid for by me as a placatory gesture, and went to meet him before the women came.

I wore the gloves that accompany this letter, which were laden with the paste of Wolfsbane obtained from Shenzen on my last visit. I rubbed his hands thoroughly with it, knowing he had a weakened heart and it would cause seizures and death.

I am writing this letter to confirm that Bagla killed Bonny and I am solely responsible for Bagla's death. No innocent should be mistakenly incriminated for these murders.

Signed

Daniel Hong

The autumn evening had cloaked Kolkata in smoky darkness, with the hint of a chill in the air, as they pulled up to the Police Headquarters. While a few of the floors were dark, the rest of the building was blazing with artificial light and was humming with activity.

Azizi was looking for them impatiently and practically chased the team into his room, where Police Commissioner Bhattacharya himself was waiting. The commissioner's fair and aquiline features under his fashionably styled shock of white hair was crinkled in concern and he drummed the table softly with his long fingers as the investigating officers debriefed the two senior policemen.

Detective Inspectors Bagchi and Kumar presented the interlocked cases, drawing up the timelines on an evidence board that showed how everything fit together. Inspector

Kundu was able to add vital confirmation that the Dubai number belonged to Daniel Hong and that Mr Hong had taken the Emirates flight to Dubai that morning—which explained why there was a long period of silence after the first message until the second set of text messages came together in the evening.

Finally, both the commissioner and the joint commissioner seemed to accept that the overwhelming evidence was incontrovertible. The team was dismissed with a stern admonition not to speak of the matter to anyone, not even their families, because the commissioner would consult with the chief minister in the morning before releasing a statement.

Pradyot was the last to leave as the commissioner put an arm around his shoulder reassuringly. "This is really a terrible business, terrible for the families, for the wider business community and for our beloved state. I wish this had happened somewhere else, I really do—but, it did happen here, we have to accept it as what it is. The only good thing is the energy and diligence with which you got to the root of the matter, Pradyot. It was not easy, I know, well done, well done."

"Yes, good work, Banerjee," echoed Sikander Azizi. "But you need to be prepared for the aftermath, you know. There will be intense media scrutiny and all sorts of messages from related and unrelated people and even personal attacks. Of course, the departmental resources are all here to help you deal with it—but you need to be mentally prepared," he advised while parting.

It was almost midnight when Pradyot drove back into the large family bungalow in Ballygunge, but unsurprisingly, his mother was still awake; she roused the waiting servants to set out dinner for her beloved son. He realised how famished he was as he tucked gratefully into the hot food while his mother asked him a series of questions and then tried to answer them herself, most of them about his health and willingness to get married.

Later, fully fed and showered, he pensively watched the waves of moonbeams break as they went through the lace curtains in his bedroom, to scatter in silvery fragments all over the floor, changing slowly into his nightclothes.

He should have been elated at the manner and speed in which he had cracked open his first major case; and he did indeed feel a tired sense of satisfaction, but it seemed somehow superficial. He could not quite shake off a niggling feeling deep inside, a shadow of a doubt, a whisper from his subconscious self perhaps, that something was missing.

He tossed and turned in his bed for quite some time, rethinking the events of the day to settle his nerves and convince himself that everything had indeed fallen into place correctly, but as he could not spot any mistake, his tired mind and body at last gave up on the quest as he dropped off into slumber.

When he woke up with a start sometime later, he realised he was sweating lightly despite the chill of the massive split air conditioner streaming cold air into the room. He looked at the luminous dial of his watch, which told him it was 4.30 in the morning.

His heart was thudding in his chest.

He knew what he had been missing.

Despite the hour, he got up and got dressed quickly. On his way down, he called Inspector Kundu's number, which was answered after several rings by his very sleepy wife. Despite the grim situation, he was forced to grin at her icy disapproval as he told her where he needed the Inspector to meet him.

The night drive was swift, as there was little traffic on the roads which were eerily lit by streetlamps that looked a hazy yellow through the early morning fog. Darkened building sped away on both sides of him as he raced through.

Inspector Kundu arrived at the Joyous Dragon a few minutes after Pradyot, looking absurdly fresh and alert, his normal cheerfulness undiminished. Pradyot had had time to wake the watchman and the servants, who had informed Allie Lim that ACP Banerjee wanted to meet her, so the door had already been opened for them. Inspector Kundu followed at a more sedate pace as Pradyot bounded up the stairs to the living quarters on the third floor.

Allie was seated primly in the drawing room, wearing a dull crimson silk dressing gown with high collars and long sleeves over a long nightdress, her expression showing part exasperation, part apprehension. She had clearly been waiting for a few minutes. She did not rise to greet them, but looked expectantly at ACP Banerjee.

Inspector Kundu settled down on a low settee to take notes, while Pradyot paced nervously around the small room, making it feel even smaller.

"I am genuinely sorry to have to do this, Mrs Lim. But I have to chase down the truth," he said in a gentle voice as he finally stopped in front of Allie. "In the beginning when I first met you, I mistook your excessive overclothes as a cover for a skin issue, but unfortunately, the signs are quite clear now—you faced domestic abuse at the hands of the deceased Mr Lim. There are residual bruises on your face and arms, which is why the high collars and the long sleeves in this weather; and there is some testimony from the servants which we will investigate in further detail, which touched upon this aspect… But very sadly, Mrs Lim, it does not stop there."

Pradyot took a deep breath, he felt really bad for Allie. "Mrs Lim, I now believe that Mr Lim's violence and possibly sexual domination extended to your daughter Linda as well. This is not a wild allegation, Mrs Lim, I have met and interviewed victims of sexual predators in my training days and Linda has all the classic signs, including the bruising and the overclothes like you. I have in fact asked for a female medical team to examine both of you, they are on their way over and should be here anytime now."

Allie had initially straightened her back in indignation when he had started to speak, but as he continued, she slowly crumpled back into the high-backed chair and seemed to collapse into herself, hugging herself with her arms and slowly rocking back and forth.

"I do not know when Mr Lim's molestation of Linda started or how far it had gone, but I believe on the evening of Diwali, you reached a breaking point. You could bear it no more and you used possibly your father's gun to shoot Bonny Lim dead as he was on his way to Linda's room. Your pent up anger and hurt exploded at that time, which explains the multiple bullets emptied into his face. You did not stop shooting after he was dead, you did not stop shooting until you emptied the contents of the gun. That in itself is a classic response of a victim of sexual violence."

Large glistening teardrops were starting to gently roll down Allie's face now and her rocking was slightly more pronounced, a few long, slow, shuddering sobs mingling with her breathing now, but her eyes were still fixated on Pradyot's face.

He looked at her for a long moment and then continued gently, but relentlessly, "Once the enormity of your actions sank in, you telephoned your father, who is a clever and resourceful man, one who was determined to protect you at any cost. We have the records of the call from the telecom company, we are looking to see if there is a shadow recording of it. In any case, Mrs Lim, the call from you to your father proves that your alibi was concocted, that you were not at your father's house with him." He knew the statement about call recordings was untrue as calls were not recorded in India, but he was hoping Allie Lim would not know this fact.

"To escape detection, you may have run down the disused spiral fire escapes at the back of all these buildings or maybe one of the secret passages between buildings which Chinatown is fabled for, but we will retrace your steps and find the clothes you were wearing, which should still have evidence of gunshot residues."

Pradyot stopped and chose his words even more carefully; from here on, the narrative was pure conjecture on his part.

"I believe Mr Hong immediately checked the guests in the private rooms as these were the people on the spot who could be seen to have the opportunity to access the living quarters. He made a list of who he could use in his conspiracy plot and then targeted Mr Bagla because of his known unsavoury past and numerous public enemies. He then arranged for prostitutes for Mr Bagla next day and carried through his plot to kill Mr Bagla with the poison, sacrificing Mr Bagla to try and save you.

"The only additional step not mentioned in his letter would be to wipe the prints off the gun and imprint Mr Bagla's prints on it, probably after Mr Bagla died. Maybe he went himself as a driver or more likely got one of his many loyal employees to impersonate a driver and put the gun with the oilcloth in the car early the next morning. No matter, we will identify the driver through an identity parade…"

Allie was weeping heavily now, accompanied by hiccupping sobs which shook her petite frame. As she spoke in a choked voice haltingly through her tears, Pradyot had to get down on his haunches in front of her to make out her words.

"You…you just don't know how it was, trying to be normal. Bonny was such a… such a horrible devil, he could be so charismatic and so kind at times but mad and lustful and out of his head at other times. I tried…I really did try my best to make it work, I knew I could survive a few beatings and make the best of it because I could not fail in another marriage, but my poor, poor Linda, my precious innocent baby… I had to protect her, I had to protect her, I am her mother, what was I to do?" she uttered in deep anguish.

There was a silence only broken by the sound of Inspector Kundu's pen on paper.

"Mr Hong, I guess he is in Dubai now, isn't he?" Pradyot asked softly.

Allie nodded through her tears.

"I guess that is because there is no formal extradition agreement with India?"

Again, Allie nodded.

Pradyot guessed a canny businessman like Hong would have money stashed away in Dubai for a rainy day, possibly have invested in another business there as well. It would probably be impossible to force him to return to India to pay for his crimes.

And yet, with a momentary twinge of deep empathy, Pradyot realised that Daniel Hong had done what most fathers always wanted to do, exactly what Allie had—tried to protect his daughter. But he had gone much farther than normal fathers would, he had taken another man's life.

Footsteps on the staircase announced Detective Inspector Kumar and the medical team. Leaving Kundu to brief them on the next steps, Pradyot massaged the back his neck with both hands and walked over slowly to the window. He knew he had to rouse JPC Azizi from his slumber and inform him that while there was still a terrible murder, they would be spared the public media spectacle of shaming a major local businessman as a murderer.

He wondered idly—would he ever be able to take another human being's life to protect his own daughter in the future?

He prayed to God he might never be put in a situation where he would have to find out.

As he dialled JPC Azizi on his mobile phone, he watched the sun slowly free itself of the far horizon and rise into the lightening skies over the darkened silhouette of Kolkata, pushing back the blanket of darkness for another day.

10

The Meeting

Dhruv Kumar only fully realised the significance of his late father's advice almost a fortnight after his passing.

It was the thirteenth day after Ajay bhai, the senior Mr Kumar, had left for his heavenly abode. The family pandit had completed the ritualistic ceremonies a little while ago. Ajay bhai's eldest son, Sushil Kumar—Supreme Court advocate and infamous protector of the rights of wealthy miners unfortunately accused of wrongdoing by an overzealous public interest litigation and an inexplicably interventionist government machinery—had offered the traditional prayers. Among those present were his two younger brothers—Dhruv and Dheeraj Kumar, proud and over-supportive son-in-law to the rich and powerful auto parts magnate, Kamal Oberoi.

The puja had been sobering and heartfelt, the completion of which had released the guests from their formal obligations, allowing them to revert to type.

The youngsters who had been emotionally blackmailed into attendance by their parents or grandparents along with a few friends of Ajay bhai's grandchildren were gathered around the dessert portion of the buffet, earnestly commencing their inevitable march towards adult diabetes. As was the unspoken norm, the teenaged boys and girls were clustered in separate groupings, with much whispering and surreptitious exchanges of glances. The only ones who crossed over the invisible gender divide were the few who had a sibling in the other group; these intrepid explorers wore their unique gender access like a badge of honour to augment their natural awkwardness in formal adult social situations.

Many of their parents had also joined in the condolence meeting, along with cousins and friends of the three brothers, but that middle generation had quickly broken up and were gathered now on the second floor of the sprawling Kumar mansion, where Sushil and his wife Pramila lived. There was another food arrangement there and some stronger liquid sustenance as well, which Ajay bhai had enjoyed during his life but which was deemed inappropriate for his memoriam at his residence.

A large group of elderly gentlemen, mostly white-haired or bald (and a few incorrigible optimists with impossibly black hair and moustaches that sat incongruously on their wrinkled complexions), had claimed the most comfortable seating area on the same floor as the puja, having willy-nilly conscripted any other piece of furniture which struck them as relaxing. The group included an assortment of Ajay bhai's cousins, his ex-colleagues, his morning walk group and a few outstation childhood friends.

When they had first entered, before the ceremony began, they had all despondently trooped past Meena-ji, Ajay bhai's widow, with heartfelt condolences, while she greeted them all calmly and sadly. Now they were sitting around regurgitating all the many shared memories of the deceased, many of them scurrilous and naughty, in their own way celebrating a life fully lived.

Their food needs were being supplied by a combined effort of all of their wives, elderly ladies who went uncomplainingly back and forth from the buffet laden with plates, with no one considering this sense of male entitlement to be unusual. Joshi saab, who was a recent widower, timidly watched while his peers started munching until Mr Talwar gestured with his eyes towards the diminutive and fiery Mrs Talwar, who immediately filled up a plate identical to her husband's and placed it in the hands of a grateful Joshi saab.

A little more segregated was the elderly women's group; three elderly widowed ladies sat on one side, positioned so that their sharp eyes and sharper tongues could capture a thousand little interactions, gestures and glances, which they then wove together to form several risqué and speculative scripts, many of which were quite alarmingly close to the truth.

Their subject at this moment was Dhruv, the youngest of Ajay bhai and Meena-ji's four children; considered by most of their friends to be Meena-ji's indulgence of her middle ages (and a sign that even with the onset of years, Ajay bhai's passion could overwhelm his caution and judgement).

"He is going to be thirty soon, I do not see how Meena can get him married well now," one of them was saying.

"Well, he is a good-looking young man… plus, he does stand to inherit this floor of the building when Meena passes… not to forget that he looks after his parents with a lot of love and care," interjected the second.

"All that is fine," said the third, brushing aside Dhruv's good qualities dismissively, "but he has done nothing with his life at all. Sushil was the clever one, he did brilliantly in college and has made such a great career finding loopholes in the law to defend his high-profile clients. And Dheeraj was never book-smart but was still sharp enough to marry into such a rich family and play his cards well. But Dhruv has just been marking time with his little construction company on small projects that do not even pay the bills…"

"He is basically like their spinster daughter," cackled the first old lady with the unabashed chauvinistic dark humour of her generation.

"Maybe you are right," the second old lady grudgingly acknowledged. "He has been protected so much that he will never be able to stand on his own feet at all…"

Behind them on the balcony where he had sneaked out for a rare cigarette, Dhruv stood silently with his hand halfway to his lips, his cigarette smouldering slowly. His day, which was already laden with grief, seemed to suddenly be enveloped in a dark new cloud, which reflected immediately on his downcast countenance.

Before he could fully ponder over what he had inadvertently overheard, he heard his mother calling out for him from one of the inner rooms. Dutifully stubbing his cigarette against the balcony railings, he went in, carefully averting his eyes from the trio gathered inside, who were suddenly silenced at his appearance.

They watched him walk away with speculative eyes, wondering what damage they might have caused.

The Kumars were a prominent family in this select neighbourhood of Delhi.

The great-great-grandfather, Kumar Amir Chand, had been a senior court official to the Nawab of Awadh, a profession which had led to his amassing great wealth. While the abolition of the monarchy had left his son Daulat Chand a wealthy migrant to Delhi, the enterprising young man had studied law in Oxford and built up a flourishing law practice with British patronage, giving him fame and allowing him to add generously to the family's accumulated wealth.

Daulat Chand had married a young lady of gentle birth and impoverished fortune, so chosen by his mother that she would be grateful for all that her in-laws could provide for her and therefore be amenable to her mother-in-law's bidding on a lifelong basis. Despite his busy legal duties, Daulat Chand and his wife gave birth to a string of four daughters, for each of whom he did his duty (including carving out a portion of the family's wealth in their names) since he was a man of principle who denied the common male-dominated patriarchal practices of the time. But he pined for a son and was delighted when at last his union was blessed with little Ajay.

Ajay being the child of much older parents was accorded a unique level of freedom and indulgence that neither his peers nor his siblings could have dreamt of enjoying. But he was a gentle-natured, dreamy scholar who never abused those privileges, a dutiful son who followed his father to Oxford but to study English rather than the more commercially focused law. He returned to Delhi to commence teaching in the most prestigious college in Delhi, which his father accepted as a starting point, expecting him to move on to more commercially impactful roles in due course.

But Ajay never left, spending a lifetime in academia and in shaping young minds, ultimately retiring as Head of Department and Deputy Dean.

Ajay's marriage was duly arranged by his mother keeping in mind the same principles that her mother-in-law had used, for this was the accepted wisdom of the times. And dreamy scholar though he was, Ajay and Meena produced two sons in quick succession—Sushil and Dheeraj. Daulat Chand was then still in the prime of his legal career, but senior enough to be surrounded by a host of senior employees in his firm who did all that he asked, so he had more than enough time to devote himself to his two young grandsons, imbuing in them strong commercial values and a fiercely competitive approach that brooked no opposition.

Although Ajay had a comfortable salary, it was not ever going to make him a rich man; and Daulat Chand felt this lack of wealth keenly, taking it as a personal failure on his part, which prompted him to do his best to impart all his accumulated years of aggression and sharp practice to his grandsons, who proved ever willing listeners, many a times shamelessly bribed by lavish gifts from their grandfather.

Dhruv was born when his eldest brother Sushil was entering law college and Dheeraj was romancing the wealthiest girl in their undergraduate class, five years after Daulat Chand had succumbed to a massive stroke, sadly followed a year later by his wife.

Dhruv was therefore raised in a different environment from his brothers, with older parents and no grandparents. Daulat Chand's practice had been sold to his other partners and while the family was still wealthy, the fame, influence and income associated with a powerful law firm with a legendary litigator leading it was on the wane. Dhruv was also lovingly shielded by older brothers from the vagaries of the world and later by his affectionate sisters-in-law. So he grew up without any pressure to compete, gentle and caring and very mindful of the many ethical lessons his scholarly father had embedded in his young psyche.

Even after he earned his double qualifications as an architect as well as a civil engineer and set up shop for himself with a small construction company, he remained laidback and adhered to the strictest moral code—refusing to bribe, pad the accounts, obtain competitor data or any of the other practices which were part and parcel of the more successful firms in the field.

Thus, Dhruv lived a serene life in his personal family cocoon—till the terrible afternoon when Ajay bhai went to sleep after lunch and never woke up.

The rest of the thirteenth day memoriam passed in busy activities, but sleep came late to Dhruv that night as he grappled with the twin loss of his father and his innocence. He remained captive to a brooding mood the entire next day, pecking at his food, refusing to even eat a full meal at his mother's coaxing.

Being a logical and fair person, he had to admit that the assassination of his character by the three old ladies was not without merit. He had in fact over the past couple of years felt mildly impatient at his own lethargy and complacence and had even sought his father's guidance on a few occasions. Ajay bhai had probably erred by reserving criticism and supportively consoling him. However, he had given Dhruv one valuable piece of advice, which he had repeated over the years.

"The major construction projects are mostly in the government sector, my son. You should go and meet the Minister for Infrastructure and Urban Development. But do not go empty-handed, go with a proposal that shows you can add value to them. Make him your ally by the dint of perseverance and the quality of your work, that is the route to success." These had been Ajay bhai's sage words.

As Dhruv sat huddled up in his room through the day, reliving the hurtful overheard conversation and thinking over the place where he found himself, his mood evolved from disappointment to slow anger, which metamorphosed by evening into a resolve to take control of his life and change it.

His father's advice rang ever more true in his mind. And by the time he went to bed late that night, he had determined that he would invest all his time in getting a meeting with the minister.

Meena-ji and Dhruv's brothers were all greatly encouraged by the turnaround in his mood the next morning and the energy and zest he showed after that.

Dhruv spent the next few weeks in preparing for the meeting, by putting together a proposal which he had long envisioned—a combined underpass and flyover in his neighbourhood crossing to ease traffic and enhance the liveability and value of the neighbourhood, right down to changes in municipal waterways, additional power requirements and rerouted sewage pipes. Since he was both an engineer and an architect, after a few weeks of intense effort, he was able to put together a first draft which he was both proud of as well as keen to present to the minister.

But he realised soon enough that putting together a plan was the easy part, getting it across to the minister was another matter altogether.

Sushil advised him firmly against sending an email, saying, "Any one in that office with access to that email will be able to read and plagiarise your idea and present it as their own. Yes, yes—maybe we could use the email evidence to reclaim the credit, but that may take years in court! How will a protracted legal battle serve your purpose, Dhruv?"

So Dhruv opted to visit the ministry complex physically, where he was unexpectedly but firmly thwarted multiple times by the primitive manual security apparatus. No matter what he explained to the haphazardly uniformed duo guarding the gateway, they would only parrot their limited instructions, "We need to confirm with the minister's office if you have an appointment…"

Of course, there was no confirmation of any appointment and Dhruv beat a hasty retreat every time.

A few months passed, with Dhruv's repeat appearances at the gate making no visible impression on the uniformed guardians of the complex.

The business tycoon's son-in-law, Dhruv's brother Dheeraj, advised Dhruv to bribe his way in. "Clearly, they are angling for some handouts, just grease their palms and you will be sitting in the minister's office in no time at all, Dhruv.

This is the time to be practical, you must do what the world is doing so that you can compete."

Dhruv, having spent his young life abiding by his father's idealistic values, did not openly disagree with his elder brother at the dinner table, but stubbornly felt a bribe would undermine everything he was trying to achieve; so, he discreetly continued looking for other solutions.

It was one of his loyal employees who finally made the wise suggestion that got him through the gates. "Sir, since we deal with so many others who visit the ministry," Suresh, the old-timer had ventured, "why don't we go along with one of them and branch off to visit the minister once we are inside?"

Dhruv was enthused by this harmless subterfuge and immediately started asking around. Although the construction company he ran was small and had only undertaken a handful of projects over a decade of being in operation, both the company and Dhruv enjoyed solid goodwill amongst those who knew them because of his scrupulous honesty. And so it was that within a fortnight of asking around, Dhruv and Suresh were seated in the back seat of a dusty white SUV at the gateway to the ministry complex.

Once inside the main building, Dhruv profusely thanked the slightly surprised architect who had brought them in and set off in search of the office of Shri Pavan Handa, the Minister of Infrastructure and Urban Development, with Suresh firmly in tow.

Visitors to the minister had to first congregate in a waiting room where various senior government officials would tend to them, leaving only the high-impact or most serious issues to be dealt with by the minister.

To gain entry to this waiting room, visitors had to be screened by Shri Handa's private secretary, a hawk-eyed, middle-aged veteran of many administrations.

And to even be able to cross the threshold of the private secretary's sprawling chambers, the peon sitting outside had to first be satisfied about the bona fides of the visitor.

Dhruv failed completely at the first hurdle.

No matter his persuasive arguments, Chuni Lal had seen thousands of supplicants before—eager ones, clever ones, the rich, the stupid and the criminal ones. And as he sat in his crisp beige government-issue uniform and dispensed access to the private secretary through paan-stained lips, he was able to correctly divine that there was little value in Dhruv meeting the minister.

Dhruv was forced to retire, baffled.

It was now more than six months since his father's passing.

During this period, apart from his pursuit of a meeting with the minister, Dhruv had also been attacking his work with renewed zeal to quote for every piece of business that he could. His renewed activity caught his small team by surprise, but most of them had been with him since he started the business a decade ago, and were intensely loyal to their quirkily honest master and so they threw themselves into the work with him. They had seen him forgo his profits, pay salaries from his personal savings and even pawn his Rolex watch (a graduation gift from his parents) during lean times rather than lay off any employee, which bound them together in ways that no legal contract ever could.

But the big projects and the government tenders continued to elude them, since they neither had a track record and nor would they bribe key decision makers.

Of the many projects they had bid for, the Sharada Charitable Hospital, the new school from the Bhasin Trust, the new block of government apartments and a few other big construction contracts were yet to be awarded, allowing Dhruv to remain cautiously optimistic despite still awaiting the meeting which would set his career on the fast track.

As he explained to his mother, who had started talking about the need to find a good girl and get married, he needed to do something first, be someone, achieve something.

After being so easily dismissed by Chuni Lal, Dhruv tried to rethink his approach. He searched high and low for any common acquaintance who could introduce him to Minister Handa, but no one amongst his family and friends had ever been in the construction or infrastructure domain, so he drew a blank. Left with no other choice, he girded his loins and went back in full force to tackle Chuni Lal, this time formally dressed for the boardroom, carrying a portfolio of his past work and credentials, with freshly printed impressive business cards.

Dhruv asked the same favour again of the business contact who had driven them in the first time. That kindly gentleman offered to connect Dhruv to some agents who could get him into the minister's proximity for a fee and rolled his eyes when he was treated to a lecture on probity. Nevertheless, once again, he drove Dhruv into the ministry complex, accompanied by the faithful Suresh.

Chuni Lal unfortunately remained unimpressed by Dhruv's effort at professional formality. Dhruv felt the peon's wrinkled old eyes dismissing him… "We have seen so many like you come and go," they seemed to be saying.

Whilst he was pleading his case, Suresh tugged at Dhruv's suit sleeve. "Sahib, someone is waving at you."

Dhruv looked up distractedly to see the neighbourhood busybody Vir Singh, one of his neighbours, at the other end of the corridor, trying to attract Dhruv's attention. Dhruv made a respectful gesture of namaste, which seemed to be all that the effervescent middle-aged Mr Singh was looking for.

Vir Singh, queueing between various government departments required to obtain the permit he was seeking, was a wealthy, social human being who was inquisitive to the point of being nosy, loved technology toys and was terribly keen to always be the first with any news. It was second nature to him to whip out his iPhone and click a picture of Dhruv in front of the minister's office and send it to Dhruv's elder brother Dheeraj through the medium of their early morning walkers' WhatsApp group, with the caption: "Youngest of the Kumar brothers is now stalking the corridors of power!"

Thus having gently violated the privacy of multiple people with some fresh-off-the-oven news, Mr Singh went back happily to the task of providing the government with inky fingerprints on multiple documents.

Dhruv on the other hand unhappily beat a retreat, his waves of optimistic arguments shattering on the implacable cliff of Chuni Lal's indifference. He stood despondently for a long moment, then started walking away slowly.

As he neared the end of the long corridor, he realised Suresh was not with him. He looked back to see Suresh handing Chuni Lal a piece of paper and gestured to him impatiently.

"What was that? Did you give him something?" He asked as Suresh jogged slowly to join him.

"He wanted your address, so I wrote it down for him…" Suresh explained, breathing heavily.

Dhruv stopped in his tracks. "Are you sure? Why would he want that? You were not bribing him, were you?"

Suresh took his boss's arm and gently guided him towards the exit, saying with affectionate sarcasm, "Yes sahib, you are right, while our owner is selling his watch to pay our salaries, I have made enough money to throw it around government offices."

Dhruv grinned despite himself and allowed himself to be led away, still wondering why a government peon would want his address.

The mystery was answered a few days later, when an invitation to attend Chuni Lal's son's wedding was delivered to the Kumar household. Dhruv was puzzling over why he was invited at the breakfast table when his mother gently explained it to her naïve son.

"This man controls access to the minister's office na, beta? I guess he has invited people who deal with the minister or who wish to deal with him, hoping for some lavish gifts under the pretext of this family occasion, maybe even significant sums of money, which would otherwise arouse suspicion if he accepted them within the ministry…"

Dhruv was somewhat indignant that anyone could think he would deliver cash bribes at a wedding, but after discussions with his brothers and consulting his senior employees, he realised it would potentially antagonise Chuni Lal if he ignored the invitation, so he decided to attend the wedding.

"Besides anything else," he said to Suresh as they drove to the wedding together carrying a modest and appropriate silver bowl as the gift, "I should not prejudge the fellow. Maybe he is better than we suspect. Maybe we will meet the minister at the wedding?"

Suresh made a disbelieving noise but did not argue with his idealistic boss as Dhruv's driver skilfully navigated through narrow winding lanes.

They arrived to find a fiercely lit up location crammed with people.

After a quick look around, Suresh turned to Dhruv. "Sahib, this occasion does not match your stature. As far as I can see, it is only people at my level who are here, none of the owners have come, you are the owner and you should go back…"

Dhruv looked around himself and acknowledged the truth of Suresh's observation, but he was already here and he felt it would be disrespectful to set foot in the venue and then turn away, which his innate decency would not allow.

To formally register their presence with him, they searched through the rooms of the hired venue for Chuni Lal, finally locating him in a flustered discussion with his close family. Apparently, the designated groom's wedding horse had been injured at the last minute. Even though the bride's home was just a few hundred metres away and Chuni Lal's invitees would all walk there behind the groom, for the groom to arrive on foot was not only inauspicious, it would undermine Chuni Lal's standing in the community.

Dhruv and Suresh stood inside the partially opened door and listened to the heated argument about alternatives. Dhruv could sense the extreme stress in the room, especially Chuni Lal's frustration as a father, and his decent soul felt the need to help. He stepped forward and cleared his throat. "Hrrrmph… er…. Excuse me," Dhruv blurted out, much to Suresh's consternation. "You can use my car…"

There was a sudden silence as everyone turned to look at him. Most looked puzzled by his presence as no one knew him except Chuni Lal, across whose face astonishment chased hope.

And so it was that after half an hour, the groom was waving to everyone while standing up through the sunroof of Dhruv's Mercedes, while a brass band belting out Bollywood music preceded them, with a large crowd of dancing friends and relatives swarming all around the car, followed sedately by the more formal invitees and assorted non-dancers.

The entrance to the bride's home was an unmitigated triumph for the groom's family and the wedding proceedings got underway with due pomp and ceremony.

There were a number of customary photographs, with Chuni Lal insisting that Dhruv and Suresh have pride of place in them. Once they learnt that the minister would not be attending as he was travelling out of town, Dhruv and Suresh stayed till the wedding began and then politely made an early exit.

Minister Pavan Handa, being a kind man who cared for his co-workers, tweeted his good wishes to Chuni Lal's family overnight, with a photograph of the whole family in their wedding finery. Unbeknownst to Dhruv, the photo displayed Dhruv standing awkwardly next to a beaming Chuni Lal.

As Dhruv came down early the next morning for his walk, he was in for a surprise.

Chuni Lal was seated in the watchman's cabin, waiting for him, looking worn out with happiness, still dressed in the now crumpled finery of the previous night. Before Dhruv could say anything, Chuni Lal bowed deeply in front of him with folded hands. "So many rich and powerful people speak to me, they see me as an instrument for their needs, a lowly tool, someone to pay off. You have treated me as a human, as an equal, as a friend… You allowed me to hold my head up during my daughter's marriage… I can never repay you…" he said in a choked voice, his eyes suddenly swollen red with tears.

Dhruv held Chuni Lal's hands in both of his and patted the older man on the back reassuringly, feeling embarrassed by the other's overwhelming gratitude. Then he gently led him back to the house for a comforting cup of tea.

Om Prakash Bhasin, patriarch of the wealthy Aurangzeb Road Bhasin family and chairman of the Bhasin group of companies, was addressing the final meeting of the trustees of the Bhasin school to decide the construction of their new school, their biggest yet.

"There are the two shortlisted companies, both established firms." He gestured to the binders lying on the conference table. "But I was really interested in this other proposal from a smaller firm, owned by a Dhruv Kumar," he said, holding another binder in his hand. "They have proposed the lowest cost and are committing the fastest delivery—but I do not know whether they can deliver what they promise…"

He passed the binder around the room. "I would be very interested to know your views please?"

Senior Supreme Court advocate, Mrs Sunita Kapoor, was the first to glance through the document and comment, "I think this is Sushil Kumar's brother? Sushil is a senior colleague of mine at the Supreme Court, I know them, they are a very prominent family."

"Oh, he is that Dhruv Kumar? Then he is very well connected to the Ministry for Infrastructure and Urban Development," chimed in the diminutive Madhav Pathak, who was part of Sushil Kumar's and Vir Singh's morning walk group. "I have seen photographs of him at the minister's office all over WhatsApp…" he completed in rhetorical exaggeration.

Professor P.K. Sinha, who was an architect by training, was flicking through the binder thoughtfully. "This seems very detailed … robust planning," he shared thoughtfully. "And I have some personal experience of this firm—they had built an additional floor for my sister and they were scrupulously honest, completed well on time."

Om Prakash Bhasin was silent, gazing contemplatively at the collection of binders on the table, as they all turned back to him for a decision.

Chuni Lal's newfound devotion resulted in Dhruv and Suresh once again smuggling themselves into the ministry complex with their now openly amused business contact. Chuni Lal thrust aside the line of supplicants to escort them through to Minister Pavan Handa's private secretary, a long-serving, middle-aged civil servant whose ash-lined forehead told the story of his disciplined tryst with his Divine every morning before work.

M.S. Manisubramaniam heard Dhruv out impatiently and broke in with his strongly accented Hindi, "Yes, yes—I am sure the proposal is great, but the minister does not evaluate individual proposals, kannaa. Why aren't you sending an email? Or a physical document? Then it could be evaluated through the proper channels and if it is worthy of further consideration, it will be recommended to the minister…"

Dhruv was mindful of his elder brother's strictures about plagiarism and was thus highly reluctant to share his prized proposal with any intermediary, so he tried to gently remonstrate with Manisubramaniam; but to no avail. The experienced and knowledgeable civil servant quickly sent Dhruv packing, wordlessly conveying that many other important matters of state were being impeded by these immature and pointless arguments.

However, Dhruv did not have the opportunity to brood for long, as the sudden and unexpected awarding of the huge Bhasin school project overjoyed his entire team (and his family) and enveloped them in a flurry of frenetic activity round the clock to drive the construction of this project of unprecedented size for their little firm.

Even with all their exceptional efforts and the various subcontractors to whom parcels of the work were handed out, Dhruv's little firm found themselves woefully short-handed. So Dhruv started to recruit architects, engineers and administrative staff. With no reputation and limited funds, he hired a bunch of raw youngsters with absolutely no experience, which proved to be a blessing in disguise as it infused fresh young energy which meshed very well with the experienced group of original staffers.

A lingering concern at the back of Dhruv's mind was how he would keep the larger new team fully occupied once the key milestones of the Bhasin project were met.

But he need not have worried.

The laying of the foundation stone of the project was converted into a flamboyant media event by the Bhasin Group's PR team. To add to the publicity storm, various senior members of the Bhasin Group took to Twitter as well as Facebook—all of it with photos prominently highlighting Dhruv's firm.

This publicity was lapped up by interested eyes, which led to robust enquiries about new projects, nowhere as large as the school project but larger than they had been handling earlier, keeping them all busier than ever before.

Meena-ji was happy for her youngest, but she worried about the pressures of his lifestyle, about his day-to-day stress and about his single-minded devotion to his work. Her maternal view was firmly that he did not have the secure companionship his brothers enjoyed in their married lives. So she took the marriage discussions further with him, by coaxing him to see the photographs and profiles of various young eligible women every chance she got.

But Dhruv's first and driving priority was the Bhasin school project. During the ensuing months of frenetic activity, Dhruv planned quite a few times to renew his pursuit of the elusive meeting with Minister Pavan Handa, but some last-minute glitch always claimed his attention as the entire project moved forward at great pace.

And so it transpired that a short seven months after commencement, the senior members of the Bhasin Group management and the family were once again gathered to launch the administrative centre of the school, which had been completed in record time.

Afterwards, Mr Bhasin drew Dhruv aside into the empty principal's office in a conspiratorial manner, along with another venerable senior citizen somewhat overdressed in traditional clothes, whom he introduced respectfully.

"This is Raja Sumer Singh sahib…" began Mr Bhasin, but the other gentleman affectionately smacked Mr Bhasin's hand aside and spoke with warmth, "Our privy purse has been banished for decades, I don't know why this damn old man accords me more respect than I deserve," he said laughingly. "We have known each other for all our lives now…

"The thing is, son," he continued, "my family runs the Sharada trust, which is building our first speciality hospital in Delhi. We have commenced the project, of course, where we have been now struggling for several months with unkept promises and fluctuating costs…"

Dhruv listened silently, a wild hope beginning to form in his mind.

"Om Prakash and his entire senior management team speak very highly of your firm and of you, son," Raja Sumer Singh said, turning serious. "You've done quite a job here, and really, your integrity of effort has won everyone's trust completely. You are the kind of firm we need on our charitable venture, someone who will take the job seriously and do it well. Someone with old-fashioned values and purity of intent."

"Not to forget his influence in the ministry," interjected Mr Bhasin, eager to ensure that his protégé received all the credit due to him.

"I know," concurred Raja sahib. "I saw that Minister Handa's Twitter feed even had Dhruv's photographs."

And thus, one of the largest private construction projects in the national capital was awarded to Dhruv's growing little firm.

Dhruv and his team were tremendously excited about this huge new contract, but they approached it with a high degree of caution.

The key issue was simple—they had inherited a mess.

The earlier firm had misread the city planning documents and as a result, their entire design and architecture was based on laying foundations that would damage the existing municipal water and sewage lines. After poring over the plans for almost a month and a long, hard honest conversation with the Sharada Trustees, Dhruv and his team came up with some workaround options, with inevitable attached costs, but solutions that would get the job done. The Sharada Trustees debated and questioned the changes over a couple of hectic days and finally agreed, much comforted by the fact that Dhruv's honest calculations led him to confirm he could bring the project in almost at the same time and within the same cost that the original contractor had promised.

But the big concern was the approval from the Ministry of Infrastructure and Urban Planning.

Given the complexity, Dhruv was highly optimistic that this was definitely the opportunity to present his case personally to the minister.

M.S. Manisubramaniam was even more definite this was not something that needed the minister's personal attention.

"This is a routine approval," he proclaimed, after flicking through the file. "Any senior functionary in this office can approve it." He looked shrewdly over his half-moon glasses at Dhruv. "You think you have to bribe someone to get all these changes approved, don't you?"

Dhruv shifted uncomfortably under the other's reproachful gaze.

Manisubramaniam made an exasperated sound. "What is wrong with you people? Can't you see the progress being made in infrastructure and civil construction all around us? Would that happen if we were constantly holding up the work for bribes?"

At Chuni Lal's request, Manisubramaniam consented to write the name of a senior bureaucrat on the file. "There, he can take care of it."

"Er… Sir…how long will it take? When do you think it can be reviewed?" Dhruv asked hesitantly.

"Uff… OK, relax, young man, I will telephone him now," responded Manisubramaniam, taking pity on the earnest, honest man in front of him who had been pursuing a meeting with his political master for almost two years now. "A call from the minister's private secretary ensures prompt action. Besides," he added wryly, looking up over his half-moon spectacles, "elections are coming up. Handa-ji's instructions are to clear all proposals swiftly so that the value of this government can be felt by all."

Raja Sumer Singh was overjoyed a mere fortnight later to learn that the revised plans had been so expeditiously approved. He eased his ample girth out of his imposing lush leather armchair to hurry around his table and hug the embarrassed young man in front of him. "This is amazing, absolutely wonderful!" He declared. "OP was damn right, you are not just a great architect, your influence with the ministry is something quite special!"

Dhruv's native honesty prompted him to object, pointing out that the Ministry had delivered without any influence required, but Raja sahib was already celebrating, calling his family and thanking Om Prakash Bhasin on the phone.

Dhruv made a mental note to remind Raja sahib of the good work of the ministry at a more propitious moment.

During this extremely busy period, Meena-ji tenderly forced Dhruv to take a day off to accompany her to the marriage of the son of one of Ajay bhai's closest colleagues. She explained that she needed to lean on Dhruv emotionally when facing so many people who had been so close to his father, at which he had swallowed his reluctance—but to his surprise and annoyance, she disappeared in a sea of acquaintances within minutes of arriving at the event.

Dhruv was brooding at the ubiquitous bar, when his mother reappeared with a much younger lady in tow.

"Beta, you remember Poornima, Professor Dikshit's daughter? You used to play together when your fathers were starting out as assistant professors in the college?" Meena-ji turned to Poornima. "Dhruv has been asking about you, you know… Chalo, I shall leave you both to catch up…" Saying this, she meandered off gently, waving to someone.

Poornima quizzed Dhruv with her hazel intelligent eyes. "Asking for me? Do you even remember me?"

Dhruv cast around in his mind for a reassuring and clever reply but he heard himself blurt out, "You used to have those ugly steel braces…"

Poornima's eyebrows snapped together as she replied tartly, "Really? And your little shorts inherited from some older brother were always falling off!"

There was a brief silence, then they broke into embarrassed laughter together.

"Truce," offered Dhruv, holding out his hand, feeling an inexplicable elation as she grasped his hand and dimpled back at him.

Poornima was also a professor, teaching in one of the renowned girls' colleges in Delhi, a woman of strength and substance. The middle sibling of three, Poornima had travelled the world and had survived an early unhappy marriage. Dhruv found her easy to talk to and easier to miss when she was not around.

They had a wonderful, wide-ranging conversation, which began that night and carried on through shy exploratory telephone calls, through hesitant meals at posh restaurants and at roadside dhabas, through passionate political debates and through long drives together when he picked her up from her college and took a detour around Delhi before he dropped her back.

Until one day, when Meena ji announced to the gathered family over dinner, "I have invited Professor Dikshit and his family over this Sunday. We need to decide some dates. I want all of you to be there please to support me."

There was immediate good-natured banter aimed at Dhruv by both his brothers as well as his elder nieces and nephews, but both his elder sisters-in-law looked at him doubtfully as they half-expected him to object again. Indeed, the first phase of Sharada Hospital had been launched earlier that week and the media coverage was great, with Dhruv and his firm being accorded pride of place by Raja Sumer Singh. So another busy period of growth was very much in the offing for his fast-rising firm and it would have been in character for Dhruv to object to any personal commitments at this time.

But Dhruv carried on eating in exaggerated silence, trying hard to look unconcerned, as the banter quickly degenerated into bawdy jokes around him.

That Sunday, the entire Kumar family dressed in their best to formally greet and welcome the Dikshits as they trooped in together, accompanied by a thick-set older gentleman with heavy eyebrows and a bustling air of energy, whom Mrs Dikshit introduced as her brother.

"He was my first boyfriend and he needs to approve of you," Poornima teased Dhruv with a smile as she introduced them.

"I see from the media that you are a stalwart in the construction business, son. You must come and meet me, we need firms like yours..." Minister Pavan Handa said with a smile as Dhruv bent to touch his feet, suddenly feeling Ajay bhai's presence and blessing all around him.

11

All in the Stars

Close to the famous trading city of Paithan, in a small and picturesque village called Sauviragram, which lay not far from the banks of the powerful Godavari, lived a young woman called Ilaa.

Being cotton farmers (as most in that region were) with a sizeable holding of land, her family was well to do, quite the richest in their village and even their zilla.

It was the harvest season now, and cotton had to be plucked laboriously by hand from the plants. There was a frenetic energy in the plucking activity because the wholesalers and traders from Paithan would be arriving in just a few weeks, carrying gold coins and goods for barter. They would exchange what they carried for the best cotton that the farmers grew so that it could be taken back to the mills of Paithan and woven into fine cloth to be sold up and down the length and breadth of Hindustan, including the bulk buyers of the East India

Company. The bales of cotton had to be ready in time; entire families joined in the harvesting efforts, masters and servants alike—work was at its peak.

Even though her entire family was involved, Ilaa was not to be found in the fields today. Instead, she had wandered far from the fields on a cloudless, sun-drenched morning and was sitting by the banks of the great river Godavari on a little hillock, as a stray breeze blew strands of her long hair around her head.

"I am sick of this!" she declared in a trembling voice to no one in particular. She took a couple of hiccupping breaths and then brushed the tears away from her face in an angry gesture with the back of her hand as she tried to control the angry sobs that welled up inside her.

Ilaa's had been a short but eventful life up to that moment.

Born to an impoverished Paithan nobleman, Vishnu Digamber and his beautiful third wife, Manasi, seventeen summers ago, Ilaa had been considered a divine boon by her mother. Vishnu Digamber had married Manasi late in life, smitten by her luminous beauty, her harried and caring parents happy to see one of their many daughters married to a noble family, no matter how poor.

Vishnu Digamber had no experience of the vagaries of life, as he had lived off the inherited landholdings of his ancestors all his adult life. His personal share of the inheritance, fragmented by division across generations, might have reduced his income to a fraction of what his forebears enjoyed, but that did not deter him from sowing his seed freely. His first two wives had dutifully presented him with three and two sons respectively—unfortunately loutish and unthinking lads whose future their despairing father rightfully predicted as grim.

Hence, by the time he brought home a young Manasi, the ageing and chastened Vishnu Digamber had had his fill of male heirs.

"These boys will have to share a meagre inheritance between so many of them already..." he gently told his new bride. "To add to which, we know they are not capable of growing our family's name or wealth any further... I think it is time to ask Ganpati for a daughter, someone who will marry well into a powerful family and resurrect our fortunes..."

A few months passed after the consummation of their marriage without Manasi conceiving. Since she considered this her primary duty in her marriage, this made her increasingly restless until one day she gifted away all her personal worldly possessions and prostrated herself before the revered sand idol of Bhagwan Munisuvrat Nath, the famed holy site in Paithan where once Ram and Sita had also prayed. If it ever occurred to her that her respected husband's advanced age could be a deterrent to conceiving a child, she never spoke of it to anyone, not even in a whisper in her mind to the gods.

And Manasi's unbending faith rewarded her, because on a silken starlit summer night nine months after her prayers, Manasi's proud womb gifted Ilaa to her doting father.

From the moment she first smiled with a new-born's sightless and toothless gaze at her father, Ilaa could do no wrong in his eyes. Vishnu Digamber's wrinkled eyes misted over when he first held her. "She is here, my beautiful little princess is here, the mighty Lambodar has blessed us..." was all he could say.

Ilaa was granted exceptional and unusual privilege for a girl child of the times, as her father flouted all the conventions of her times by allowing and encouraging her to study with her much older brothers, where she excelled and sometimes even bested them in male-dominated subjects like philosophy, mathematics and logic; she often snuggled up to her father in the lengthening shadows of the evenfall while he narrated epic tales of Vedic times, getting him to repeat stories of Parvati, Savitri, Damayanti, Draupadi—legendary and mythical female figures who fired her girlish imagination.

She had a most unique gift of reading body language and spotting liars—a gift with which she first earned her brothers' wrath and later their grudging admiration as she was able to tell on them to her father and their mothers whenever they refused to admit to their misdeed; and which helped her father successfully conclude the transactions of the many family heirlooms which an impoverished nobleman had to sell in order to meet his family obligations.

Ilaa was only eleven when a much touted travelling conjuror arrived to perform at the Raj Mahal in Paithan. Since the overlord of Paithan was a benevolent and clever man who understood the value of keeping his flock engaged and happy, the entire nobility of the city along with their families was invited to view the wondrous skills of the visitor.

While everybody was spellbound at how he was making Rudraksha beads appear and disappear under upturned gold cups, little Ilaa suddenly ran out from behind the curtain which protected the women from public view and pounced on one cup. "It is here, it is here," she exclaimed, bouncing on her feet and clapping her hands in excitement, her long hair dancing in waves around her.

The turbaned and grandly dressed prestidigitator smiled tightly and speeded up his sleight of hand, but Ilaa stood happily in front of him and outguessed the bemused man on every move—spreading unseemly hilarity through the youngers in the gathered crowd. By the time Manasi had gathered her daughter back behind the purdah, the hapless conjuror's reputation lay in shreds.

The beautiful, spirited and clever little girl was noticed by many seeing eyes that day, most especially by a wealthy old cotton grower from Sauviragram, Jnaneshwar Sindhu, who sought a private meeting with her father through intermediaries known to them both, to ask for Ilaa's hand in marriage. "You have many wives yourself," Jnaneshwar reassured Vishnu Digamber. "You know how valuable the youngest can be. I will treat her like my queen, she will want for nothing at all. And neither will her family," he continued meaningfully, looking into Vishnu Digamber's eyes.

Vishnu Digamber grappled manfully with his dilemma for a few days. On the one hand, his pride and deep affection for Ilaa held him back from trading his beloved daughter to a man older than himself; on the other, his by now creeping penury and the combined pressure of his two elder wives forced him to reconsider the rich suitor.

Ilaa was almost twelve when she entered Jnaneshwar Sindhu's extended household, which included her husband's two earlier wives, their children, his younger brothers and their family and even Jnaneshwar's mother—a shrivelled, ancient termagant with sharp eyes and a sharper tongue who considered Jnaneshwar the centre of her universe, and who controlled the entire household with an iron fist.

Ilaa was given over to the old lady as soon as she stepped over the threshold of her new husband's house, where she lived under her mother-in-law's protection and tutelage in the inner sanctorum of the house that was the women's preserve till she reached puberty at fourteen. When she first met the old martinet, Ilaa prostrated herself before her mother-in-law as her mother had advised, only looking up shyly to agree in childish innocence and awe as Jnaneshwar's mother extolled his many virtues, real and imagined.

"He is so magnificent," Ilaa breathed, not really having experienced men beyond her gentle father and loutish brothers. "Your ladyship, let me serve you, teach me to be worthy of him," she finished, thus unwittingly winning over her first and most powerful ally.

During those years till she was ready to join her husband in his bed, Ilaa stayed loyally by her mother-in-law's side, ever ready to learn and support. Ilaa's confident energy and intellect, nurtured by her father, asserted itself as she slowly built a reputation as an efficient organiser of the many household servants, a flawless bookkeeper and very importantly, someone who was almost impossible to deceive—but always deferring to and supporting her mother-in-law, as Manasi had trained her to be. As she matured, she grew ever more beautiful, lovingly groomed under her mother-in-law's eyes by skilled servants as the old lady wielded this bright and biddable girl as a weapon against her elder daughters-in-law from Jnaneshwar and his brothers.

Based on the many reports from his mother, Ilaa thus already had Jnaneshwar's surprised respect when she finally was deemed of age to consummate her marriage; the presence of this beautiful, strong and clever girl in his bed, along with his mature years, made him a hesitant and somewhat inept lover. But Ilaa in her innocence accepted his ineffectual fumbling as his gentle love and responded confidently with all the pent up passion of her fourteen years, making him happier than he had ever been before.

"I have waited for you all my life, you are the one dearest to me," he repeatedly told her, privately at first and over time in front of other family members (other than his mother), as the rest looked at each other surreptitiously with various expressions ranging from annoyance to scorn to downright jealousy.

Jnaneshwar spent almost all of his time with his youngest bride and took to sharing anecdotes of his business dealings when they sat together in the lamplight at evenfall. Ilaa listened comfortably in the beginning, but soon her irrepressible nature exerted itself and she offered him her comments, which surprised Jnaneshwar with their insight.

He soon started coming to her for advice. The next three years saw Ilaa grow to be Jnaneshwar's right hand in business with her unique skills, wielding increasing authority, although always from behind a purdah. She did not bear children during all this time, which gave her some concern, but Jnaneshwar had two sons and three daughters from earlier wives, so he was willing to wait for his child bride to conceive.

Until one day, he did not wake up in the morning.

And Ilaa's little world suddenly fell apart around her.

She realised within hours how dependent she and Jnaneshwar's mother had been on the continued beating of Jnaneshwar's heart. She was not even allowed time to grieve but was swiftly stripped of her finery, shorn of her locks and banished to a room next to the servants, to be fed late in the day on food left over from the family repast. As Jnaneshwar's sons swiftly took control and their mothers and wives ensured their own benefits in a disintegrating domestic order, Ilaa found over the coming days and weeks that she had no money, no authority, no rights, no voice and no life…because she had become a childless widow at seventeen.

Ilaa tried to contact her parents in the first few awful days, but Paithan was almost a full day's ride away and no servant would make the journey without being suitably compensated. Within a month of her intolerable new life, Ilaa could bear it no more. She ran away to the banks of the Godavari outside the village, vaguely planning to end her life.

As Ilaa blinked through her tears at the sun-dappled valley below her, her agitated mind was momentarily diverted by the sight of an English Army battalion, snaking its way along the cart tracks from Paithan. This sight triggered a sudden happy memory, which flashed uninvited in her mind's eye.

It had been two months earlier that the visiting English colonel had brought his educated captain, a short, wiry young fellow whom everyone called 'Tiny', to lecture the village elders on astronomy. Entranced by Tiny's vision of a heliocentric universe, Ilaa had once again forgotten herself and called out from behind the purdah on the upper floor, "So why do the stars not fall upon the earth like fruit? What holds them up?"

In the ensuing confusion, Captain Tiny's startled hazel eyes had locked with her warm brown ones for an interminable moment. But there were village elders upset at this breach of protocol, an angry colonel bristling at the unjust interrogation by an unschooled native woman, amused children suddenly running amok and a bustle of women disappearing hastily to their domestic duties to avoid involvement, so no answer was possible.

Captain Tiny and his faithful batman did call next day at Jnaneshwar's haveli to explain that he had no explanation—yet. But he never got past the superficial pleasantries with the menfolk in the outer courtyard, which guarded the inner sanctorum of the women with a wall stronger than brick and mortar.

Thinking back to that day, desperate and unhappy as she was, a windblown seed of an outrageous plan started to grow in Ilaa's mind…

❧

Captain Tiny did not discover the stowaway for almost two days. It was only while his batman was pulling off his boots on the second night that Tiny found himself once more looking into oddly familiar luminous brown eyes in the mirror, peering out from the giant wardrobe in his caravan.

His trepidation was battling with his curiosity when she disarmed him completely by asking, "Have you seen a falling star yet?"

They talked animatedly through the night, of astronomy and death and her plight and his ambition and of nothing at all as well; and then they slept, childlike, through the next day. Her limited English and his faltering Hindi barely reached out across the yawning chasm between their two cultures, but their sparkling attraction built a connection between them that was as old as time.

The camp gossip reached the colonel before Captain Tiny could. It was too late to turn back to Sauviragram, so the colonel gave in to Tiny's pleas on her behalf and gruffly instructed Captain Tiny to "Keep the wench, but be discreet—I don't want to fight off a posse of natives just before I return you safely to London."

By the time they reached the coast, the strength of their companionship had taken the entire camp by surprise—especially when their unbidden guest spent long hours not only listening to Tiny's many abstract theories but apparently understanding enough to engage him in spirited debate after that. So much so that it seemed only natural that Ilaa would return with Tiny at the end of his army stint to Cambridge, which had been shut to cleanse itself of the plague—a closed period which had allowed Tiny the opportunity to explore the wonders of India through a junior commission bought in the British Army.

A few days later, as her heart beat faster watching her own land disappear from the ship's windows, Ilaa's mind was almost overcome with the myriad memories of the life that she was forsaking to step into the unknown; but then there was Tiny, who had told her, "Whatever you can dream of, we can work to make true together. You will be respected and loved and protected, my dearest." He had also said, looking deep into her eyes, "All the questions that you have, all the study that you want to pursue, will be made possible by the greatest intellectual resources in the world…"

Tiny's intense passion and gentle care quickly helped settle her as the ship made its month-long journey towards England, offering Ilaa a solace and a relationship she had never known before. All the while, her agile mind and her constant companion worked together to polish her spoken English.

By the end of the journey, Tiny knew that he was not going to be able to share his life with anyone else ever again. But he knew better than Ilaa that the echelons of English society to which he and his family belonged would never recognise, far less accommodate, their relationship. So, as soon as they landed, Tiny took Ilaa to live with his indulgent and loving grandmother Margery Ayscough in Woolsthorpe as her companion while he returned to earn a scholarship in Trinity College, Cambridge.

The old lady was absolutely delighted to see her youngest grandson back, whom she had raised from infancy after his mother remarried. Having seen a lot of life, she did not ask questions about his light-eyed, long-haired companion, now dressed in a smart dress and bonnet from London, but waited to be told about her.

"I want you to be happy, dear boy. Not like your poor father, who was so unhappy with your mother that he died young before you were even born—God rest his soul," she said at last when Tiny finished explaining, sitting at her feet as he used to during his childhood. "But the girl has to become a Christian, I am not having a heathen in my house, neither will the townspeople stand for it."

In truth, Margery was sadly lonely, other than the farmhands on her property, and she realised that with Ilaa in the house, her beloved grandson would be drawn back there as long as his affection lasted; all the while giving her a companion to lighten the loneliness, heathen though her origins might have been.

Ilaa was duly converted to Christianity. She kept her thoughts to herself and responded sensibly to Tiny's supportive comments, although she wept inwardly and in the privacy of her room at the loss of her roots. For her part, the old lady treated Ilaa kindly and they found a mutual meeting ground of affection, but Ilaa only ever fully came to life every time Tiny walked in the door, filled with passion and love, discussing his theories and hypotheses with her.

He shared his work freely and sometimes stayed more than the weekend, debating, postulating, challenging each other. They returned frequently to her question about the stars, and while she did not fully follow him through all the unmapped terrain that his mind was traversing, she did realise that observing nature together in their orchard was confirming his ideas and somehow helping him build a bridge of knowledge for future generations to walk upon.

Ilaa never did have children, but Tiny never loved or respected her less. As his prodigious and growing body of philosophical work in logic and mathematics earned him fame and accolades, he treasured even more the private moments they had together.

And in the ultimate recognition of his incredible career, when Queen Anne came to Trinity College to knight him, Ilaa was the only guest he had eyes for. Captain Tiny smiled with rich contentment when Ilaa pointed mischievously at the stars as Her Majesty placed her Royal Sword on his shoulder and pronounced, "Rise, Sir Isaac Newton."

Author's Note: Isaac Newton was studying in Cambridge when in 1665, the university closed down for two years to cleanse itself of the plague, forcing students to return to their homes or pursue other activities. There are no records of his having ever married or having a relationship with anyone, although there has always been speculation as to why.

Acknowledgements

My parents, like all parents, gave me hope, self-belief, unending love and the confidence that I could tell a story. Every good thing that I am or could be, is because of them, my thanks will never be enough to tell them what they mean to me.

I have to thank my schoolteachers in La Martiniere Calcutta (as it was then), who unfailingly encouraged me, for which I am eternally grateful.

I am grateful to my friend and senior (in every sense), the intensely creative and ridiculously well-organised Bhaswar Mukherjee, for showing me the way.

Thanks to all the members of my school WhatsApp groups for affectionately cheering every silly limerick, which fuelled the fire to write through the long years in a corporate avatar.

The warmest of thanks to my agent Suhail Mathur, who is a wise guide, a deeply knowledgeable partner and an always optimistic co-traveller; and to the wonderful people at Om Books, led by the gentle erudition of Shantanu Ray Chaudhuri, for bringing this little anthology to life and allowing it to be presented to the world.

Thanks to our multifaceted son, the beat of my heart, who is a stern and realistic critic. And to his strong and talented mother, the gentlest and most uncritical of all, who is the very sunshine that lights my soul.

And last, but not the least, my thanks to the reader for picking up a copy. I hope you enjoy reading it as much and more than I did writing it.